The McKinsey Global Institute

The McKinsey Global Institute (MGI), established in 1990, is McKinsey & Company's business and economics research arm.

MGI's mission is to help leaders in the commercial, public, and social sectors develop a deeper understanding of the evolution of the global economy and to provide a fact base that contributes to decision making on critical management and policy issues.

MGI research combines two disciplines: economics and management. Economists often have limited access to the practical problems facing senior managers, while senior managers often lack the time and incentive to look beyond their own industry to the larger issues of the global economy. By integrating these perspectives, MGI is able to gain insights into the microeconomic underpinnings of the long-term macroeconomic trends impacting business strategy and policy making. For nearly two decades, MGI has utilized this "micro-to-macro" approach in research covering more than 20 countries and 30 industry sectors.

MGI's current research agenda focuses on three broad areas: productivity, competitiveness, and growth; the evolution of global financial markets; and the economic impact of technology. Recent research has examined a program of reform to bolster growth in Europe; Africa's economic potential; debt and deleveraging; the impact of multinational companies on the US economy; technology-enabled business trends; urbanization in India and China; and the competitiveness of sectors and industrial policy.

MGI is led by three McKinsey & Company directors, Richard Dobbs, James Manyika, and Charles Roxburgh. Susan Lund serves as MGI's director of research. MGI project teams are led by a group of senior fellows and include consultants drawn from McKinsey's offices around the world. These teams draw on McKinsey's global network of industry and management experts and partners. In addition, MGI works with leading economists, including Nobel laureates, who act as advisers to MGI projects.

The partners of McKinsey & Company fund MGI's research, which is not commissioned by any business, government, or other institution.

Further information about MGI and copies of MGI's published reports can be found at www.mckinsey.com/mgi

McKinsey Global Institute

December 2010

Farewell to cheap capital? The implications of long-term shifts in global investment and saving

Richard Dobbs
Susan Lund
Charles Roxburgh
James Manyika
Alex Kim
Andreas Schreiner
Riccardo Boin
Rohit Chopra
Sebastian Jauch
Hyun Min Kim
Megan McDonald
John Piotrowski

Preface

Farewell to cheap capital? The implications of long-term shifts in global investment and saving is the latest research by the McKinsey Global Institute (MGI) on the outlook for global capital markets in the wake of the 2008 financial crisis and subsequent recession. Among the lingering effects of the downturn are the very low real interest rates that prevail around the world at this time. However, as global GDP growth begins to rebound, two critical questions for many businesses, consumers, investors, and governments are whether they should expect capital costs to remain low for the foreseeable future and if not, how will they be affected by rising interest rates.

In this report, we examine past trends in saving, investment, and capital costs around the world. We also look ahead, projecting investment trends and comparing them with plausible saving patterns over the next two decades under a number of different scenarios. We see that while a three-decade decline in global investment helped drive real interest rates down to their precrisis lows, an impending global investment boom may drive rates higher over the next two decades. In coming years, we may have to say farewell to cheap capital.

MGI leaders Richard Dobbs and Susan Lund directed this research, with contributions from Charles Roxburgh and James Manyika. Alex Kim and Andreas Schreiner led the project team, which comprised Riccardo Boin, Rohit Chopra, Sebastian Jauch, Hyun Min Kim, Megan McDonald, and John Piotrowski. Jonathan Ablett, Alan FitzGerald, Geoffrey Greene, Soyoko Umeno, and other members of MGI Economics Research provided valuable research support. The team would like to thank former McKinsey colleagues Bryan Cheong, Chris Crittenden, and Ankur Gulati, and MGI communications and operations professionals Tim Beacom, Deadra Henderson, Nell Henderson, and Rebeca Robboy for their many contributions.

Distinguished experts outside of McKinsey provided valuable insights and advice. In particular, we would like to thank Martin N. Baily, the Bernard L. Schwartz Chair in Economic Policy Development at the Brookings Institution; Barry P. Bosworth, the Robert V. Roosa Chair in International Economics at the Brookings Institution; Richard N. Cooper, the Maurits C. Boas professor of international economics at Harvard University; and Nobel laureate A. Michael Spence, professor of economics at the New York University Stern School of Business.

We benefited from numerous discussions with academic experts, regulators, and practitioners in the field. These include Don Argus, formerly of BHP Billiton; Serkan Arslanalp, of the International Monetary Fund (IMF); Jonathan Coslet, of TPG Capital; Udaibir Das, of the IMF; Michael Dueker, of Russell Investments; Giannandrea Falchi, of Banca d'Italia; Andrew Fleming, of Aegon Global Asset Management; Michael Klein, formerly of the World Bank and International Finance Corporation; Greg Mason, of TPG Capital; Rakesh Mohan, of Yale University; Andrew Pease, of Russell Investments; Erik Ristuben, of Russell Investments; Hyun Song Shin, of Princeton University; Adair Turner, of the UK Financial Services Authority; José Viñals, of the IMF; and Jack Weingart, of TPG Capital. While their counsel was invaluable, MGI takes full responsibility for any views expressed or errors contained in this report.

This report also would not have been possible without the thoughtful input and expertise of numerous McKinsey colleagues and alumni around the world. These include Dominic Barton, Pierre-Ignace Bernard, Tab Bowers, Marcel Brinkman Lowell Bryan, Kevin Buehler, Tim Church, David Cogman, Toos Daruvala, Miklos Dietz, Jens Dinkel, Selina Elwell, Anthony Goland, Benno Gröniger, Philipp Härle, Herbert Henzler, Jimmy Hexter, David Hunt, Bill Huyett, Bin Jiang, Conor Kehoe, Rik Kirkland, Tim Koller, Alok Kshirsagar, Nicolas Leung, Diaan-Yi Lin, Devin McGranahan, Scott Nyquist, Jeremy Oppenheim, Gordon Orr, Rob Palter, Gary Pinkus, Bruno Roy, Shirish Sankhe, Anthony Santomero, Joydeep Sengupta, Sven Smit, Elizabeth Stephenson, Michael Stewart, Patrick Viguerie, Peter Walker, Paal Weberg, Jonathan Woetzel, and Adil Zainulbhai.

Our aspiration is to provide business leaders and policy makers around the world with a fact base to better understand some of the most important trends shaping global financial markets today. We also seek to start a global dialogue on the implications of these trends among businesses, financial institutions, investors, and policy makers. As with all MGI projects, this research is independent and has not been commissioned or sponsored in any way by any business, government, or other institution.

Richard Dobbs
Director, McKinsey Global Institute
Seoul

James Manyika
Director, McKinsey Global Institute
San Francisco

Charles Roxburgh
Director, McKinsey Global Institute
London

Susan Lund
Director of Research, McKinsey Global Institute
Washington, DC

December 2010

Contents

Executive summary

The recent bursting of the global credit bubble followed three decades in which capital became progressively cheaper and more readily available. Today, interest rates remain very low for several reasons, including economic weakness in developed economies, little demand for new credit by heavily indebted households, and central bank monetary policies aimed at stimulating growth. Many people have come to believe that low interest rates now are the norm.

But our analysis suggests that this low-interest-rate environment is likely to end in the coming years. We find that the long-term trends in global saving[1] and investment[2] that contributed to low rates in the past will reverse in the decades ahead. The primary reason is that developing economies are embarking on one of the biggest building booms in history. Rapid urbanization is increasing the demand for new roads, ports, water and power systems, schools, hospitals, and other public infrastructure. Companies are building new plants and buying machinery, while workers are upgrading their housing. At the same time, aging populations and China's efforts to boost domestic consumption will constrain growth in global savings. The world may therefore be entering a new era in which the desire to invest exceeds the willingness to save, pushing real interest rates up. Higher capital costs would benefit savers and perhaps lead to more restrained borrowing behavior than we saw during the bubble years. However, they would also constrain investment and ultimately slow global growth somewhat. Among our key findings:

- The investment rate (investment as a share of GDP) of mature economies has declined significantly since the 1970s, with investment from 1980 through 2008 totaling $20 trillion less than if the investment rate had remained stable. This substantial decline in the demand for capital is an often overlooked contributor to the three-decade-long fall in real interest rates that helped feed the global credit bubble.

- The world is now at the start of another potentially enormous wave of capital investment, this time driven primarily by emerging markets.[3] We project that by 2020, global investment demand could reach levels not seen since the postwar rebuilding of Europe and Japan and the era of high growth in mature economies.

- The coming investment boom will put sustained upward pressure on real interest rates unless global saving increases significantly. In most scenarios of future

1 "Saving" refers to gross national saving, which comes from households, corporations, and governments. For households, saving is after-tax income minus consumption, so borrowing that increases consumption reduces saving. Please see the technical appendix for more detail.

2 Throughout this report, "investment" refers to gross capital investment in physical assets such as infrastructure, housing, plant, machinery, and equipment. It does not include investment in stocks, bonds, or other financial assets. Please see the technical appendix for more detail.

3 We define emerging markets as countries with average 2004-08 GDP per capita less than $14,500, excluding oil exporters. Mature economies are those with average GDP per capita at or above this threshold during this period, excluding oil exporters.

economic growth, our analysis of saving suggests that it will not increase enough, leaving a substantial gap between the willingness to save and the desire to invest.

- This difference between the demand for capital to invest and the supply of saving will likely increase real long-term interest rates. That, in turn, will reduce realized investment and may prompt more saving, bringing the two into equilibrium. We do not predict how much interest rates will increase, but we find that if they were to return to their average since the early 1970s, they would rise by about 150 basis points. And real long-term rates may start moving up within five years as investors start to price this long-term structural shift.

- These findings have important implications for business executives, financial institutions, consumers, investors, and government policy makers. All will have to adapt to a world in which capital is more costly and less plentiful, and in which more than half the world's saving and investment occurs in emerging markets. Business models will have to evolve, investors may develop new strategies, and government could play an important role in easing the transition.

FALLING INVESTMENT CONTRIBUTED TO LOW INTEREST RATES

Over the past three decades, the cost of capital has fallen, though not just for the reasons widely believed. Among the most-discussed contributors to falling interest rates was the "global saving glut"—an increase in the global supply of capital in excess of the demand for capital to invest.[4] However, we find that the glut was caused not by an increase in the world's saving rate (saving as a share of GDP). On the contrary, the global saving rate actually declined from 1970 through 2002, driven mainly by a sharp decline in household saving in mature countries.[5]

Rather, our analysis shows that the saving glut really resulted from a falloff in the demand for capital, seen in the rate of global capital investment. Since the 1970s, global investment as a share of GDP fell from 26.1 percent to a recent low of 20.8 percent in 2002 (Exhibit E 1). Total global investment from 1980 through 2008 averaged $700 billion per year less than it would have been had the investment rate of the 1970s persisted—a cumulative sum of $20 trillion. For a sense of the scale of this figure, consider that it equals the combined GDP of Japan and the United States in 2008 and that it exceeds the combined GDP of the EU-27 that year. The amount also dwarfs some other commonly cited explanations for falling interest rates. The $20 trillion is nearly four times the size of cumulative Asian current account surpluses and nearly five times the growth in money supply in excess of GDP over the period.

The global investment rate declined for several reasons. First, investment rates had soared in the decades after World War II as Japan and Europe rebuilt their shattered roads, factories, and cities. Second, since the 1960s, real global GDP growth has slowed, which lowered the need for new investment. Empirically, we see a very strong link between investment growth and GDP growth. In addition, capital goods have

---

4 Current Federal Reserve Chairman Ben S. Bernanke coined this term in a 2005 speech, "The global saving glut and the US current account deficit." In this speech, he was referring to causes of both current account imbalances—which are broad measures of trade balances—and the fall in long-term real interest rates.

5 This is based on a sample of 10 mature economies (Australia, Canada, France, Germany, Italy, Japan, South Korea, Spain, United Kingdom, and United States) and four developing economies (Brazil, China, India, and Mexico), which together accounted for about 75 percent of global GDP. A comparison of 113 countries also shows a decline in gross saving from 1980 through 2002. But, due to limited data for these countries from 1970 to 1980, we could not conduct a similar analysis comparing saving rates since the 1970s.

become cheaper relative to other goods and services over time, primarily because of rapid declines in the quality-adjusted prices of IT hardware.

Exhibit E 1

Global investment as a share of GDP has declined since 1970, with about $20 trillion cumulative less investment over the period 1980-2008

Global nominal investment rate[1] by year, 1970–2009
% of GDP, nominal values

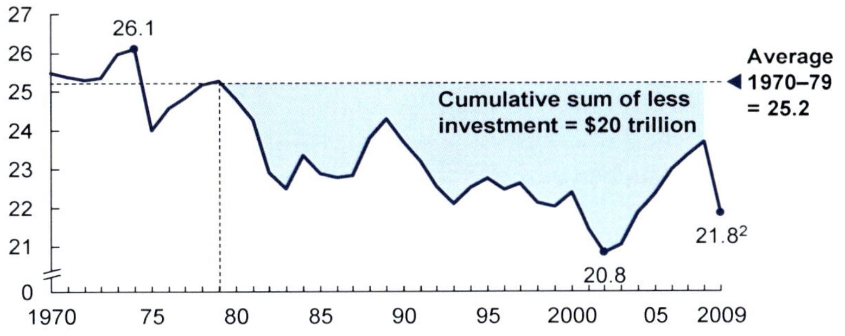

$ trillion					
Investment	0.8	2.7	5.1	7.1	14.0[3]
GDP	3.1	10.8	21.7	31.7	59.7[3]

1 Nominal gross capital formation over nominal GDP.
2 2009 data based on 53 countries.
3 2008 data (latest available figures for all countries).
SOURCE: McKinsey Global Economic Growth Database; World Development Indicators of the World Bank; Haver Analytics; McKinsey Global Institute

THE BEGINNING OF A NEW GLOBAL INVESTMENT BOOM

There have been a number of economic periods in history, such as the Industrial Revolution and the postwar reconstruction of Europe and Japan, that required massive investment. We are now at the beginning of another investment boom, this time fueled by rapid growth in emerging markets.

Across Asia, Latin America, and Africa, the demand for new homes, transport systems, water systems, factories, offices, skyscrapers, hospitals, and shopping centers has already caused a jump in investment. The global investment rate increased from a recent low of 20.8 percent of GDP in 2002 to 23.7 percent in 2008, but then dipped again during the global recession of 2009. The increase from 2002 through 2008 resulted primarily from the very high investment rates in China and India, but also from higher rates in other emerging markets. Considering the still very low levels of capital that these countries have accumulated, our analysis suggests that these high investment rates could continue for decades (Exhibit E 2).

In most scenarios of future economic growth, we project that global investment demand could increase further, exceeding 25 percent of GDP by 2030. If consensus forecasts of global growth are realized, global investment will amount to $24 trillion in 2030, compared with $11 trillion today (both figures measured at constant 2005 prices and exchange rates).[6] When we examine other scenarios for global growth, we find that investment will still increase from current levels, though less so in the cases of slower GDP growth.

6 The "consensus" GDP forecast is an average of those by the Economist Intelligence Unit, Global Insight, and Oxford Economics.

The mix of global investment will shift as emerging market economies grow. When mature economies invest, they are largely upgrading their capital stock. Factories replace old machinery with more efficient equipment, and people make home improvements. But the coming investment boom will have relatively more investment in infrastructure and residential real estate. Consider that emerging economies already invest more than twice as much in infrastructure as mature economies (5.7 percent of GDP vs. 2.8 percent). The gap is seen in all categories of infrastructure and is particularly large in transportation (e.g., roads, airports, rail), followed by power and water systems. Going forward, we project real investment demand of about $4 trillion in infrastructure, $5 trillion in residential real estate, and $15 trillion in other productive assets in 2030 in a consensus global growth scenario (Exhibit E 3).

Exhibit E 2

Capital stock per capita in China and India is very low compared with that of developed countries

Capital stock vs. GDP per capita by country and year, 1980–2008

$ thousand, sample of selected countries, constant 2005 prices and exchange rates

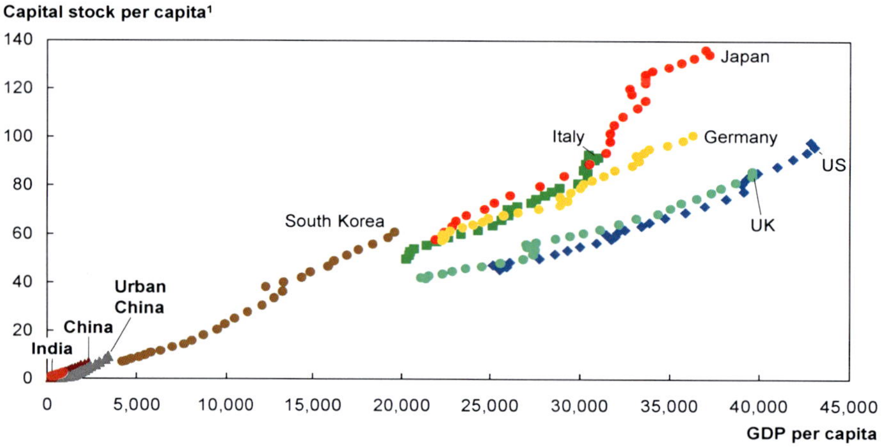

1 Stock of net fixed assets at the end of the year, assuming 5 percent depreciation rate for all the assets.

SOURCE: McKinsey Insights China; McKinsey Global Economic Growth Database; McKinsey Global Institute

Exhibit E 3

In 2030, global desired residential real estate investment is expected to reach about $5 trillion per year, while desired infrastructure investment will reach about $4 trillion

CONSENSUS GLOBAL GROWTH SCENARIO

Desired global investment[1] by industry

$ trillion, selected years, constant 2005 prices and exchange rates

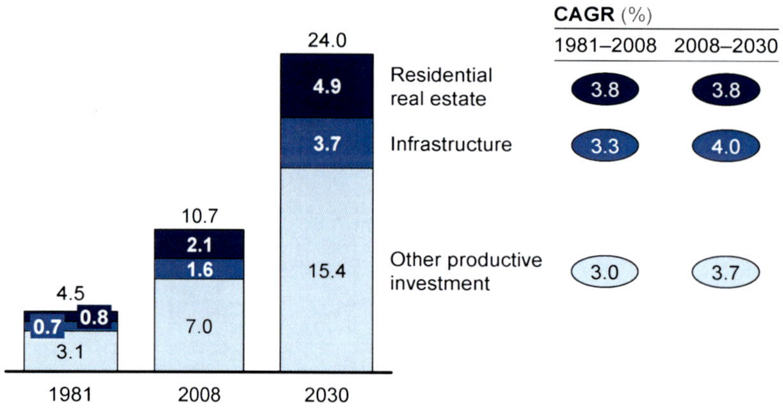

1 Forecast assumes the price of capital goods increases at the same rate as other goods and assumes no change in inventory.

SOURCE: Economist Intelligence Unit; Global Insight; McKinsey Global Economic Growth Database; Oxford Economics; World Development Indicators of the World Bank; MGI Capital Supply & Demand Model; McKinsey Global Institute

THE END OF THE SAVING GLUT

Rising investment demand will exert upward pressure on interest rates over the next 20 years if not matched by increased saving. The global saving rate has increased since 2002, but our analysis suggests that because of several structural shifts in the global economy, this trend is unlikely to continue in the two decades ahead.

First, China's saving rate will likely decline as it rebalances its economy so that domestic consumption plays a larger role in generating GDP growth. In 2008, China surpassed the United States as the world's largest saver, with its national saving rate reaching 53 percent of GDP. But if China follows the historical experience of other countries—among them Japan, South Korea, and Taiwan—its saving rate will decline over time as the country grows richer. It is unclear when this process will begin, but already the country's leaders have started to adopt policies intended to increase consumption and reduce saving.[7] If China achieves its goal, it would reduce global saving by at least 1.8 percentage points of global GDP by 2030.[8]

Another factor weighing on global saving in the future will be age-related spending. By 2030, the portion of the population over the age of 60 will reach record levels around the world. The cost of providing health care, pensions, and other services will rise along with the growing ranks of elderly. Recent research suggests that spending for the retired could increase by 3 to 3.5 percentage points of global GDP by 2030.[9] All of this additional consumption will lower global saving, through either larger government deficits or lower household and corporate saving.

There may be growth in some sources of savings in the years ahead as well. For example, households in the United States and the United Kingdom have been saving at higher rates since the 2008 financial crisis. In the United States, household saving rose to 6.6 percent of GDP in the second quarter of 2010, from 2.8 percent in the third quarter of 2005. In the United Kingdom, saving rose from 1.4 percent of GDP in 2007 to 4.5 percent in the second quarter of 2010. But even if these rates persist for two decades, they would increase the global saving rate by just 1 percentage point in 2030—not enough to offset the reduced global saving due to China restructuring its economy or countries' increased age-related spending.

All together, these trends mean that if the consensus forecasts of GDP growth are realized, the global desired saving rate will increase to around 23 percent by 2030—falling short of global investment demand by $2.4 trillion. This gap between the world's willingness to save and desire to invest will cause upward pressure on real interest rates and crowd out some investment. In turn, this could constrain global GDP growth unless the global economy can achieve higher capital productivity.

---

7 China's government officials have said publicly that increasing consumption, and hence reducing the current account surplus, will be a goal in the 12th Five-Year Plan. Also see *If you've got it, spend it: Unleashing the Chinese consumer*, McKinsey Global Institute, August 2009; or Guonan Ma and Wang Yi, 2010.

8 As with investment, this is measured in terms of 2005 exchange rates and prices.

9 "Fiscal monitor: Navigating the fiscal challenges ahead," International Monetary Fund (IMF) Fiscal Affairs Department, May 2010; and "Global aging 2010: An irreversible truth," Standard & Poor's, Oct. 7, 2010.

HIGHER REAL INTEREST RATES AHEAD

Nominal and real interest rates are currently at 30-year lows, but both are likely to rise in coming years. If real long-term interest rates were to return to their 40-year average, they would rise by about 150 basis points from the level seen in the fall of 2010, as we write this report. And they may start moving up within five years.

The growing imbalance between the world's willingness to save and desired investment will be significant by 2020. However, real long-term rates—such as the real yield on a 10-year bond—could start rising even within the next five years as investors anticipate this structural shift. Furthermore, the move upward is unlikely to be a onetime adjustment, since the projected gap between the demand for and supply of capital widens continuously from 2020 through 2030.

However, real interest rates could easily surpass their long-term average as the world adjusts to the soaring investment needs of emerging markets. Real long-term interest rates reflect the cost of borrowing, plus a risk premium to compensate investors for the possibility that inflation might increase more than expected. This risk premium could be rising today as central banks increase the money supply in an effort to spur more economic growth, creating greater investor uncertainty about future inflation.

BUSINESSES, INVESTORS, AND GOVERNMENTS WILL HAVE TO ADAPT TO A NEW ERA

Our analysis has important implications for business leaders, investors, and policy makers. Businesses and investors will have to adapt to a new era in which capital costs are higher and emerging markets will account for most of the world's saving and investment. Governments will play a vital role in setting the rules and creating the conditions that could facilitate this transition.

Business leaders must recognize that the companies that achieve higher capital productivity—output per dollar invested—will have a growing source of competitive advantage. They will need less of the costlier capital for growth, giving them greater strategic flexibility. Companies with direct and privileged sources of financing will also have a clear competitive advantage. Traditionally, this meant nurturing relationships with major financial institutions in financial hubs such as London, Tokyo, and New York. But going forward, it might also mean building ties with other large pools of capital, such as sovereign wealth funds, pension funds, and other financial institutions from the high-saving countries.

For financial institutions, the relative attractiveness of different business lines will change. Higher real interest rates may improve the economics of commercial and retail banking, which had been overshadowed by other activities in recent years. In the new era, credit volumes will likely grow more slowly as higher rates dampen loan demand, but net interest margins may go up because deposit rates typically rise less than lending rates. Maturity transformation activities will become more attractive as the yield curve is likely to become steeper than it was before the crisis. Financial institutions' capital market activities may also grow more rapidly as the largest corporations increasingly raise funds in debt markets, because they are less costly than bank loans. Moreover, midsized companies will increasingly seek access to the capital markets given the higher cost of bank lending in light of new capital standards.

Investors will want to rethink some of their strategies as real long-term interest rates rise. In the short term, any increase in interest rates could mean losses for bond holders. But over the longer term, higher real rates will enable investors to earn better returns from fixed-income investments than they could in the years of cheap capital. This will reverse the shift away from traditional fixed-income instruments and deposits toward equities and alternative investments, other things being equal. Rising real interest rates also could reduce the value of equities as the resulting higher real discount rate lowers the net present value of future cash flows. For some companies, this fall in valuation could be partially offset by a reduction in the net present value of future pensions and other liabilities.

Governments will need to encourage the flow of capital from the world's savers to the places where it can be invested in productive ways, while minimizing the risks inherent in closely intertwined global capital markets. Mature market governments need to find ways of promoting more saving and domestic investment, rebalancing their economies so they depend less on consumption to fuel growth. Policy makers in these countries, such as the United Kingdom, the United States, South Korea, and Spain, should start by putting in place mechanisms to raise household saving. Higher interest rates, by themselves, will likely curb household borrowing, which could increase net household saving. But governments should do more. They could, for instance, increase allowances for tax-free saving plans, automatically enroll workers in pension plans (with the right to opt out), and raise the retirement age.

Governments can contribute to raising gross national saving through measures to reduce their deficits, such as by cutting their own expenditures. However, governments alone could not close the projected gap between global saving and investment demand. To replace consumption as an engine of economic growth, governments in these countries also should adopt measures aimed at addressing domestic investment backlogs. To support this, they need to change from government accounting methods that treat necessary investment as consumption. When judging fiscal discipline, lawmakers, financiers, and international bodies, such as the IMF, should look at government gross saving in addition to the fiscal budget balance.

In emerging markets, governments should promote the continued development of deep and stable financial markets that can effectively gather national savings and channel funds to the most productive investments. Today, the financial systems in most emerging markets have a limited capacity to allocate savings to capital users. We see this in their low level of financial depth—or the value of domestic equities, bonds, and bank accounts as a percentage of GDP or wealth.[10] Policy makers should also create incentives to extend formal banking and other financial services to their countries' entire populations.

At the same time, policy makers around the world should create the conditions to enable long-term cross-border funding. This will require removing constraints on cross-border investing, such as restrictions on pension funds and other investors or on capital accounts. They need to ensure that tax and corporate governance systems provide more equal treatment of debt over equity. In addition, policy makers should work on creating a long-term regulatory framework for infrastructure funding. And they must create the governance and regulations that enable managers of investment funds with long-term liabilities (such as pension funds, insurance companies, and sovereign wealth funds) to focus on long-term returns and not quarterly results that reflect market movements and which can deviate from their long-term valuations.

10 See *Global capital markets: Entering a new era*, McKinsey Global Institute, September 2009.

□ □ □

As we write this report, global investment already appears to be rebounding from the 2009 recession. The outlook for global saving is less certain. A climate of costlier credit would challenge the entire global economy and could dampen future growth. However, higher interest rates would be welcomed by savers and could prevent a return to the conditions that fueled the credit bubble. Financial institutions will have to adapt and innovate as more saving and investment occurs in emerging markets. Non-financial companies will have to boost their capital productivity and secure new dedicated sources of funding as capital becomes less plentiful. While leaders must address the current economic malaise, they must also continue laying the groundwork and creating the conditions for robust long-term growth for years to come.

1. A new view of the "global saving glut"

Since the early 1980s, both nominal and real interest rates have fallen for borrowers around the world. Among the reasons often cited for this trend are loose monetary policies, central banks that have kept inflation in check, and a so-called saving glut, particularly in Asian economies.[11] However, our analysis shows that another major factor, though often overlooked, was a three-decade-long decline in capital investment as a proportion of global GDP: from 1980 to 2008, the world invested $20 trillion less than it would have, had the investment rate of the 1970s persisted.[12] This lower demand for capital contributed to lower long-term interest rates, which in turn boosted household borrowing and spending and contributed to declines in the global saving rate. The result was the great global credit bubble that burst in 2008.

1.1 THE DECLINE IN GLOBAL CAPITAL INVESTMENT WAS EQUIVALENT TO $20 TRILLION OVER THE PAST 30 YEARS

Economic growth requires continuous investment to maintain, upgrade, replace, and expand physical assets. Through capital investment, firms increase their capacity to produce goods and provide services, governments and the private sector build the infrastructure necessary to support increased economic activity, and workers upgrade their homes. Without sufficient investment, as we see in many places around the world, production breaks down, roads crumble, bridges collapse, and families live with inadequate power, water, housing, and schools.

The total value of nominal investment around the world has increased over time.[13] However, when we look at investment as a share of GDP, we see this "investment rate" has actually declined for most of the past 30 years. Capital investment fell from a peak of 26.1 percent of global GDP in the 1970s to a low of 20.8 percent in 2002[14] (Exhibit 1). As a result, total investment around the world from 1980 through 2008 was on average $700 billion per year lower than it would have been had the investment rate of the 1970s persisted—a cumulative amount of $20 trillion.

---

11 Current Federal Reserve Chairman Ben S. Bernanke coined this term in a 2005 speech, "The global saving glut and the US current account deficit." In this speech he was referring to the causes of both current account imbalances and the fall in long-term real interest rates.

12 We use the 1970s as the starting point for our time series because it is only since then that we have sufficient data from enough countries to draw conclusions about the global investment trend.

13 Throughout this report, "investment" refers to gross capital investment in physical assets such as infrastructure, housing, plant, machinery, and equipment. It does not include investment in stocks, bonds, or other financial assets.

14 The investment rate rebounded after 2002, reaching 23.7 percent of global GDP, and then dropped to 21.8 percent in 2009 because of the financial crisis and recession. The rate in the developed countries recovered partially in 2010. We discuss the trend since 2002 in the next chapter.

Exhibit 1

Global investment as a share of GDP has declined since 1970, with about $20 trillion cumulative less investment over the period 1980-2008

Global nominal investment rate[1] by year, 1970–2009

% of GDP, nominal values

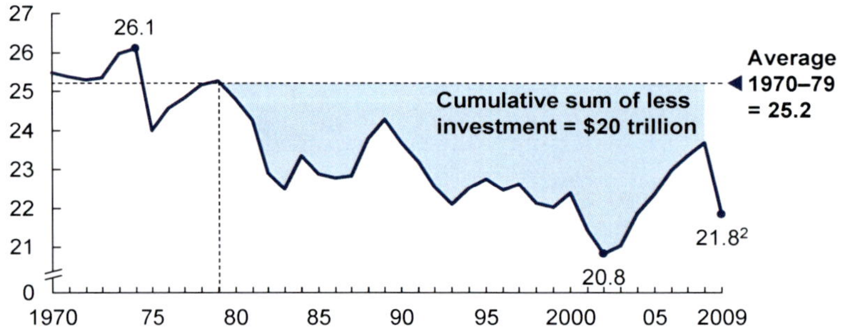

$ trillion	1970	80	90	2000	2009
Investment	0.8	2.7	5.1	7.1	14.0[3]
GDP	3.1	10.8	21.7	31.7	59.7[3]

1 Nominal gross capital formation over nominal GDP.
2 2009 data based on 53 countries.
3 2008 data (latest available figures for all countries).

SOURCE: McKinsey Global Economic Growth Database; World Development Indicators of the World Bank; Haver Analytics; McKinsey Global Institute

Maturing economies accounted for the decline in the global investment rate

The falling global investment rate reflects several trends in mature economies: the end of post-World War II rebuilding, the slowing of global GDP growth, and a fall in the cost of capital goods.

The Second World War left much of Japan and Europe in rubble. In the following years, their investment rates rose rapidly as they rebuilt their cities and industries, and as their economies recovered (Exhibit 2). By the 1960s, Japan's investment rate had reached nearly 35 percent of GDP and Germany's had reached almost 29 percent of GDP. Investment rates rose in France and the United Kingdom as well, although not by as much.

Exhibit 2

Declining investment in developed economies reflects the ebbing of a post-WWII investment boom in Western Europe and Japan

Investment rate by country—10-year periods from 1870–2008

% of GDP, nominal values

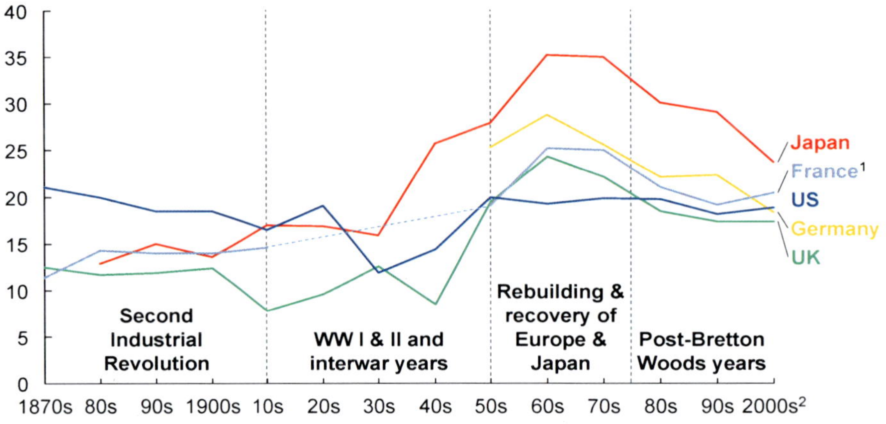

1 Data not available from 1914–49.
2 2000–08.

SOURCE: Madisson (1992); McKinsey Global Economic Growth Database; McKinsey Global Institute

By the 1960s, postwar reconstruction was complete and real global GDP growth began to slow. In the mature economies, GDP growth fell from 5.3 percent per year in the 1960s to just 2.0 percent over the period 2000–08 (Exhibit 3). Slower economic expansion, in turn, required less investment (see sidebar: *The link between growth and investment: The "rule of 2.5"*). By 2008, after three decades of slowing economic growth, Japan's investment rate had fallen to 23 percent of GDP and Germany's to 19 percent. Investment rates in France, the United Kingdom, and other parts of Europe fell as well. Because these countries accounted for such large shares of the global economy during this period, the overall global investment rate declined.

Exhibit 3

Real GDP growth has slowed in the developed countries since 1960

Real GDP compound annual growth rates, 1960–2008

%, constant 2005 prices and exchange rates

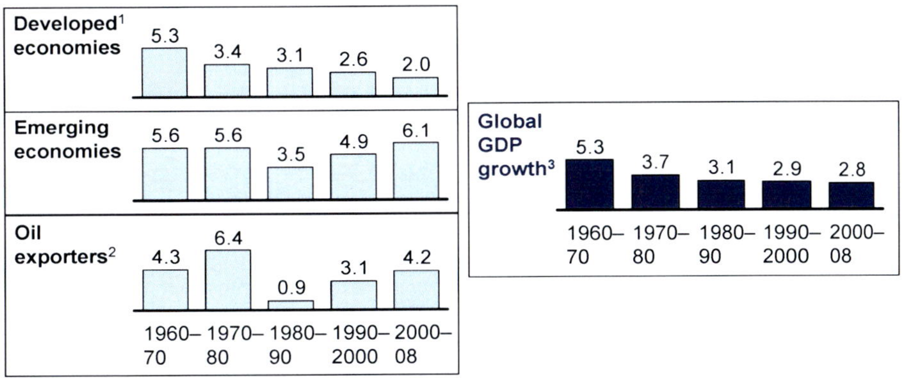

1 Countries with average 2004–08 GDP per capita greater than $14,500 (world average) excluding developed oil exporters.
2 Algeria, Angola, Azerbaijan, Bahrain, Iran, Kazakhstan, Kuwait, Libya, Norway, Oman, Qatar, Saudi Arabia, Syria, Venezuela, and Yemen.
3 Based on 67 countries with data available from 1960 through 1970, and 76 countries with data available since 1970.

SOURCE: McKinsey Global Economic Growth Database; World Development Indicators of the World Bank; McKinsey Global Institute

The link between growth and investment: The "rule of 2.5"

Across countries, there is a very strong empirical relationship between a country's investment rate and its GDP growth rate. To understand the reason for this linkage, consider the ratio of a country's stock of physical capital assets to its GDP. For most countries, this "capital-output ratio" ranges between 2 and 3, with an average of around 2.5 (Exhibit 4). Interestingly, this ratio does not seem to change much as the economy gets richer. Instead, differences depend on the productivity of investment, the quality of investment, and the mix of industries in a particular economy.

Using this ratio, we can do a rough calculation of how much investment an economy needs to support growth. One percentage point of additional GDP growth requires additional investment of 2.5 percentage points of GDP if the capital-output ratio is to be held at a constant 250 percent. This implies that countries that grow faster than others need higher rates of investment, in the same way that a growing company needs to invest more.

In addition to investment for growth, countries—like companies—must maintain their current capital stock as it depreciates. Economists estimate a depreciation rate of 5 to 6 percent annually for physical capital,[15] which implies an annual investment of roughly 14 percent of GDP to renew assets as they become obsolete or unproductive (assuming the country's capital-output ratio is 250 percent). Putting these two figures together provides a rough estimate of what a country's investment rate will be. For the United States, real GDP growth of 3 percent implies an investment rate of around 20 percent—reasonably close to the 18 to 20 percent actual rate of investment.[16] China's real GDP growth of around 10 percent implies an investment rate of around 39 percent—which is about 5 percentage points less than the actual rate of 44 percent. In fact, the capital-output ratio in China is higher than that in the United States, which in turn could be explained by a number of factors, such as underinvestment in capital in the United States, lower capital productivity in China, lower accumulated depreciation in China, measurement issues, or the composition of investment.

The "rule of 2.5" assumes a constant marginal productivity of capital: this means that each unit of capital stock added produces the same amount of output as a unit of the existing stock. Empirically, though, we see a small increase in the capital-output ratio of most countries over time.

Exhibit 4

Across countries, the physical capital stock is typically two to three times GDP

Capital-output ratio vs. GDP per capita by country, 2007

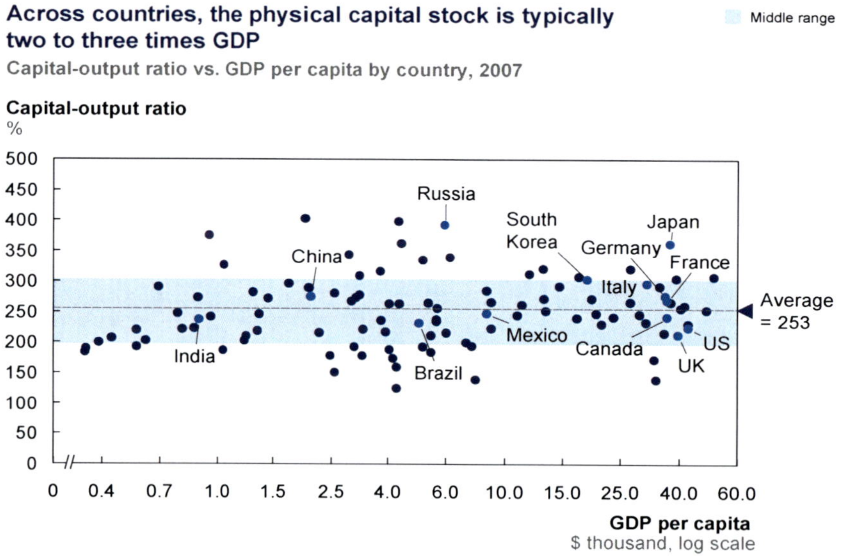

SOURCE: McKinsey Global Economic Growth Database; McKinsey Global Institute

15 For example, see Terrones and Cardarelli (2005); and Caselli and Feyer (2007).

16 For the United States, the calculation would be 3 x 2.5 = 7.5, and then add 14 for depreciation, to reach 21 percent.

In contrast to Europe and Japan, the United States maintained a stable investment rate at around 18 to 20 percent of GDP over the entire postwar period (and indeed in most years since 1870, except during wars and the Great Depression). Many economists and policy makers have worried that the US investment rate is too low. But since the 1970s, the US rate would be much higher, and indeed higher than Germany's, if we adjusted for investment in intangible capital (such as education, research and development, and brand advertising), which is not counted as investment in the national accounts. However, including investment in intangible capital—which has been stable since 1970—in our analysis would not have changed the overall decline in the global investment rate (See sidebar: *Accounting for investment in intangible capital*).

Accounting for investment in intangible capital

The definition of investment in the national accounts was developed in the 1940s, when investment in productive capacity mainly meant infrastructure, buildings, and machinery. But in today's knowledge economy, this definition no longer suffices. Instead, companies and governments can invest in "intangible assets" such as research and development (R&D), education, and brands that will increase output in the future, just as would a road or factory machine.

Including investment in intangible assets would have lifted the US investment rate to around 30 percent of GDP in 2008, rather than the recorded 18 percent (Exhibit 5).[17] This is higher than Germany's investment rate (also counting investment in intangible capital) of 28 percent. Investment in intangible capital is far less in China, at around 5 percent. However, although counting intangible capital would raise the overall investment rate, doing so would not have changed the downward trend in the global investment rate since the 1970s. This is because investment in intangible capital has increased just slightly over time.

Exhibit 5

Accounting for intangible capital lifts the US investment rate by more than 10 percentage points from 1970 to 2008

US investment rate including investment in "intangibles," 1970 through 2008

% of GDP, nominal values

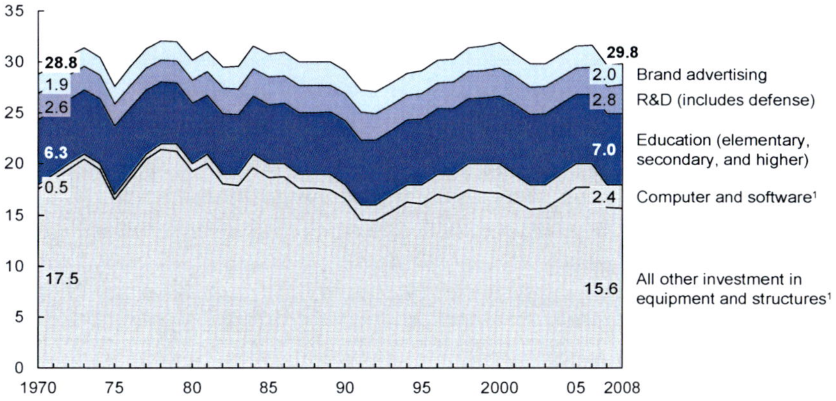

1 Counted in the national accounts as investment.

SOURCE: McKinsey Global Economic Growth Database; US Bureau of Economic Analysis; US National Science Foundation; McKinsey Marketing Practice; McKinsey Global Institute

17 This is a relatively conservative estimate of investment in intangible capital. For an alternative estimate, see Corrado, Hulten, and Sichel (September 2009).

The declining price of capital goods

Another reason the global investment rate has declined since the 1970s in nominal terms is that capital goods have become cheaper relative to other goods and services over time. This resulted primarily from rapid advances in computing power, which translated into large decreases in the quality-adjusted prices of IT hardware.[18] This decline in the quality-adjusted prices of IT hardware has benefited most sectors of the economy, enabling companies and governments to get more investment for their money. Falling prices of commodities may also have played a role in declining investment, as cheaper steel and other basic materials lowered the price of heavy equipment and machinery.

Capital intensity varies across countries

Within the mature economies, investment in manufacturing, infrastructure, agriculture, and mining has declined as a share of GDP since the 1970s. Meanwhile, investment in health, education, and other services has grown (Exhibit 6). This reflects the declining share of GDP accounted for by agriculture, manufacturing, and mining in these countries and the increasing share represented by service sectors.

Although many people assume that service industries require less capital investment than manufacturing, this is not always the case. It is true that economies with relatively large manufacturing sectors are among the most capital intensive. For instance, in Germany, China, and South Korea, the capital stock—such as machines, equipment, other structures, and housing—is worth 270 to 330 percent of GDP. By comparison, the capital stock of the United States and the United Kingdom, where service sectors account for relatively more GDP, is worth around 220 percent of GDP.

However, we find that differences in the share of manufacturing in GDP explain just a small part of the differences in capital intensity of different economies. This is because many service sectors today are just as capital intensive as manufacturing sectors. Our analysis shows that service sector capital intensity has increased sharply over the past two decades and that some sectors, such as telecommunications, education, utilities, health, and transportation, are even more capital intensive than manufacturing. The capital-output ratio of telecommunications is about 345 and education is around 290, for example, while manufacturing is about 150. Moreover, even the most basic local services, such as retail, restaurants, and dry cleaners, require real estate investment, even though they don't need much machinery or other equipment.

Other factors also explain the difference in capital intensity across countries. Japan's high capital-output ratio reflects a decade of large public investment projects designed to stimulate economic growth. In Germany, high standards for residential housing and other types of capital raise its capital-output ratio. In the United States and United Kingdom, lower investment in some areas, such as infrastructure, may contribute to their lower capital-output ratios.[19]

---

18 This fits with Moore's law, the prediction by Gordon Moore, co-founder of Intel, that the number of transistors on a microprocessor would double approximately every 18 months.

19 Also see Raj Agrawal, Stephen Findley, et al, "Capital productivity: Why the US leads and why it matters," *The McKinsey Quarterly*, 1996, number 3.

Exhibit 6

In developed countries, investment in agriculture & mining, manufacturing, and infrastructure declined most over the past 30 years

Investment as share of GDP by industry, 1980 vs. 2008

% of GDP, nominal values

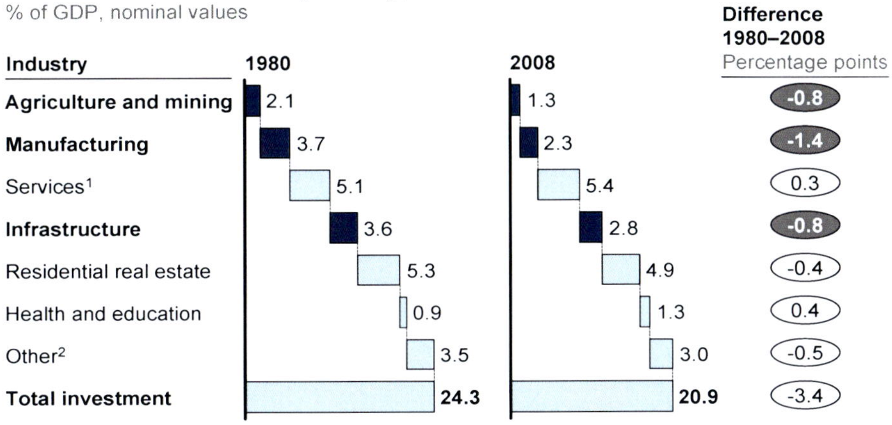

1 Includes financial intermediation, wholesale & retail trade, hotels & restaurants, leasing, business services, and real estate industry (non-residential).

2 Construction, general administration, defense & social security, social & personal services, and private household services.

SOURCE: EU KLEMS; Global Insight; McKinsey Global Economic Growth Database; World Development Indicators of the World Bank; McKinsey Global Institute

1.2 SLOWING INVESTMENT WAS A KEY CONTRIBUTOR TO DECLINING REAL INTEREST RATES

Real interest rates represent the cost of capital, resulting from the relative supply of capital (i.e., savings) and demand for capital (i.e., desired investment) at a moment in time.[20] The falling global investment rate over the past 30 years represented a significant decrease in the demand for capital—a cumulative $20 trillion from 1980 through 2008—and thus was a major contributor to a decline in real interest rates. Indeed, $20 trillion is larger than more commonly discussed sources of the global saving glut. It is nearly four times the size of the cumulative Asian current account surpluses ($5.4 trillion) and nearly five times the growth in the global money supply[21] in excess of GDP ($4.3 trillion) over the same period.

Real long-term interest rates have declined for borrowers and savers around the world since the period of high inflation in the 1970s. For example, the real yield on 10-year government bonds in mature economies declined from 8.6 percent in 1981 to just 1.7 percent in 2009 (Exhibit 7).[22] This decline in part reflects the very high interest rates at the start of the period, during which both nominal and real interest rates rose sharply. Although many people believe that inflation affects only nominal interest rates, the perceived risk of unexpected future inflation drove real interest rates higher as well. Central banks brought inflation under control in the early 1980s, but the threat of unexpected future inflation was priced into bonds for well over a decade afterward—a cautionary tale about the long-term consequences of high inflation.

20 Government borrowing is another source of demand for capital. In the national accounts, this is counted as negative saving, which affects the supply-demand balance similarly. See the technical appendix for more detail on how investment and saving determine real interest rates.

21 The global money supply is measured by M2, which comprises currency, demand deposits, traveler's checks, money in checking accounts, retail money market mutual fund balances, saving deposits (including money market deposit accounts), and small time deposits. Increases in the money supply mainly influence short-term real interest rates but can also affect long-term real interest rates through the inflation risk premium.

22 Measured by ex-post real interest rates paid on debt. See technical appendix.

While the drop in inflation expectations was one reason interest rates fell, we can see the effect of the underlying movements in the supply and demand for capital when we look at the historical yields on index-linked gilts in the United Kingdom. The yield on these bonds differs from that on conventional bonds because it does not include a premium for the risk of unexpected inflation. Therefore, the yield on these gilts can be considered the closest approximation to an ex-ante real yield. And over the past two decades, the yields on these bonds declined consistently from 3.8 percent in 1992 to 0.7 percent in September of 2010 (see technical appendix, Exhibit A 13).

Exhibit 7

In developed countries, real interest rates have fallen substantially since 1980

Long-term interest rates in developed economies

Yield to redemption on long-term government bonds,[1] 1975–2009

%, GDP-weighted

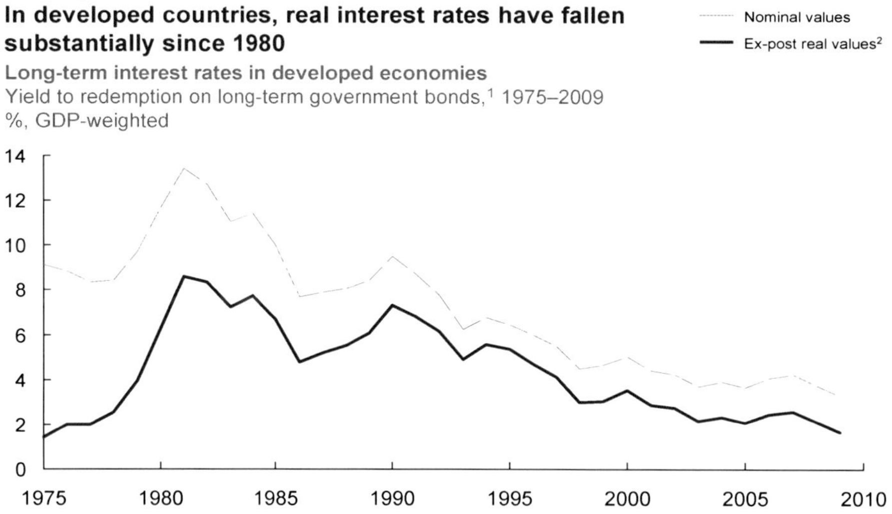

1 10-year government bonds where available. See technical appendix.

2 Calculated as nominal yield on 10-year bonds in current year minus average realized inflation over next 10 years. We use OECD estimates of inflation in 2009-19 to estimate real interest rates in 2000-09.

SOURCE: International Monetary Fund International Financial Statistics; Organisation for Economic Co-operation and Development; McKinsey Global Institute

Over the same period, government bond yields in different industrial economies have converged as the globalization of financial markets equalized returns. Back in the early 1980s, the difference in average government bond yields across Europe compared with the United States was 2.0 percentage points; since 2000, that gap has been reduced to less than 0.4 percentage points. Even more remarkable is the difference between the maximum and minimum yields on government bonds in developed countries, which fell from 16 percentage points in the 1970s to less than 3 percentage points in the years prior to the current financial crisis (although it has risen again since the sovereign debt turmoil erupted in Europe earlier this year).

A similar pattern of declining real interest rates is seen for households and corporations (Exhibit 8). Real interest rates for household debt (including mortgages and other forms of debt) in developed economies fell by half over the past 25 years, from around 8 percent in the mid-1980s to less than 3.5 percent in 2009. Most of this decline reflected lower yields on government bonds, as the spread of consumer loans over government bonds has remained remarkably stable. The cost of corporate debt fell in a similar manner.

Falling real and nominal interest rates have had many effects on the global economy and on financial markets. They helped bolster stock market performance in the 1980s and 1990s, as lower real interest rates reduced the rate at which expected future cash flows are discounted, which in turn increased valuation levels.[23] Lower interest rates also unleashed new investment in housing and commercial real estate, lifting GDP growth and employment, although not in a sustainable manner. This growth also helped boost corporate profits, as did the lower capital costs that reduced debt service payments.

However, it is now also clear that lower interest rates, excess capital, and the growth of asset prices helped fuel the global credit bubble that caused the recent financial crisis and recession. Not only did low rates make borrowing cheaper in general, but they also led banks to seek higher yields by creating new lending products and making credit more widely available to riskier borrowers. Investors bought new securitized products in an effort to boost the returns on their portfolios. Higher equity and house prices, as we will discuss later, increased perceived wealth, which encouraged greater borrowing, and the higher house prices enabled borrowers to obtain larger secured loans. As a result, debt grew around 2.3 percentage points a year faster than global GDP from 1990 to 2009. The world economy is now in the painful process of "deleveraging," or reducing this excessive accumulation of debt.[24]

Exhibit 8

Real interest rates for households and corporations have fallen since 1980, while spreads have remained fairly stable

Interest rates in developed countries

%

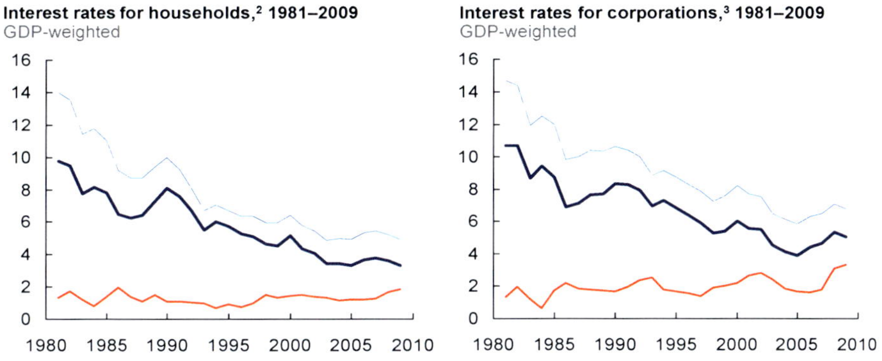

1 Calculated as nominal yield in current year, minus average realized inflation over next 10 years. We use OECD estimates of inflation in 2009-19 to estimate real interest rates in 2000-2009.
2 US 30-year mortgage; 10-year mortgage when available. See technical appendix.
3 Midgrade 10-year corporate loans when available. See technical appendix.
SOURCE: Eurostat; International Monetary Fund International Financial Statistics; US Federal Reserve; Organisation for Economic Co-operation and Development; McKinsey Global Institute

1.3 THE GLOBAL SAVING RATE DECLINED AS WELL

Based on the previous discussion, we can now see that the perceived "global saving glut" was due to the world's declining investment rate, which created an excess of saving over desired investment. Indeed, counter to what one might expect with a "saving glut," the world's saving rate did not rise. It fell from 23 percent of global GDP in 1970 to 19.6 percent in 2002. Nonetheless, declining interest rates indicate that investment demand was falling faster than saving supply.[25]

23 For a longer description of the impact of interest rates on the stock market, see chapter 7 in *Value: The Four Cornerstones of Corporate Finance* by Koller, Dobbs, and Huyett, Wiley 2010.

24 See *Debt and deleveraging: The global credit bubble and its economic consequences*, McKinsey Global Institute, January 2010.

25 If saving declined more than investment demand, we would have expected to see real interest rates rise instead of decline. See the technical appendix for more detail.

Changes in saving behavior within mature economies explain this decline (Exhibit 9). Collectively, developed countries' gross national saving fell from 22.7 percent of their GDP in 1980 to 19.7 percent in 2008. However, the pattern differs across countries. The national saving rate fell more in the United States than in any other mature country, from 20.6 percent of GDP in 1980 to 12.7 percent in 2008. In contrast, gross national saving rates were relatively stable in France and Germany.

Exhibit 9

Saving rates in developed countries have declined over the past 30 years

Gross national saving rate[1]

% of global GDP

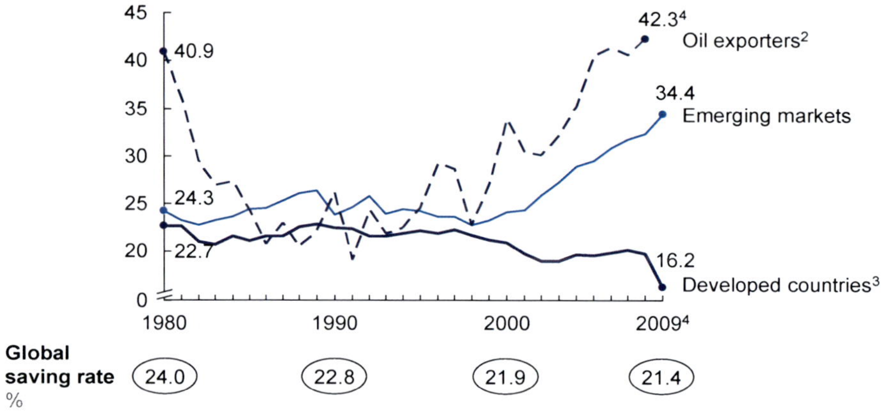

1 Gross saving by households, corporate sector, and government sector for 111 countries.
2 Algeria, Angola, Azerbaijan, Iran, Kazakhstan, Kuwait, Libya, Nigeria, Norway, Saudi Arabia, United Arab Emirates, Venezuela.
3 Countries with average 2004–08 GDP per capita > $14,500 (world average), excluding developed oil exporters.
4 Estimates based on a sample of 52 countries (equivalent to about 85 percent of global GDP); data for oil exporters through 2008.

SOURCE: CEIC; Haver Analytics; McKinsey Global Economic Growth Database; World Development Indicators of the World Bank; McKinsey Global Institute

Households explain the decline in mature economy saving

Households account for most of the drop in national saving in many developed countries.[26] The combined household saving rate fell from 12.3 percent of GDP in 1980 to 6.1 percent in 2008 in our sample of developed countries, reflecting sharp declines not only in the United States, but also in Australia, Canada, Italy, Japan, South Korea, and the United Kingdom, among others (Exhibit 10).[27]

The reasons for the decline in household saving differ across countries and are subject to some disagreement among economists.[28] One commonly discussed reason is the impact of aging populations. According to the "life cycle" model of saving developed by Franco Modigliani, Milton Friedman, and others, people should save more in their prime earning years from around age 35 through age 64 and then draw down their saving

26 Throughout this report, we use the term "saving" in its economic sense, as after-tax income less consumption. Consumption can be funded from current income, from selling assets, or from borrowing. An alternative definition of saving is household net purchases of assets less net additions of liabilities. Discrepancies between the two measures arise during periods of strong asset price movements.

27 Because of data limitations, we focus our analysis on a sample of 10 mature economies (Australia, Canada, France, Germany, Italy, Japan, South Korea, Spain, the United Kingdom, and the United States) and four developing economies (Brazil, China, India, and Mexico) since 1980. The gross household saving rate (presented as percent of GDP) includes an allowance for the consumption of fixed capital and is different from the more commonly cited "net" household saving rate (presented as percent of disposable personal income). See the technical appendix.

28 See, for instance, Horioka, 2007; Muellbauer, August 2008; Hüfner and Koske, March 2010; and Ma and Yi, June 2010.

in retirement to smooth consumption over their lifetimes. In practice, this explanation seems to fit the experience in some countries, particularly in Asia, but not others.[29] In Japan, for example, the household saving rate has declined as a growing share of the population enters retirement. But populations are aging as well in France and Germany, yet their household saving rates have not declined much and remain high, at around 10 to 11 percent of their combined GDP. In the United States, previous MGI research has found that Americans born in the first three decades of the 20th century did follow the life cycle pattern, but those born in the first decade after World War II—the early baby boomers—have not; their saving rate did not rise significantly during their prime earning years.[30]

Exhibit 10

Household saving rates in many developed countries have declined substantially

Household gross saving rates, 1980–2010

% of GDP

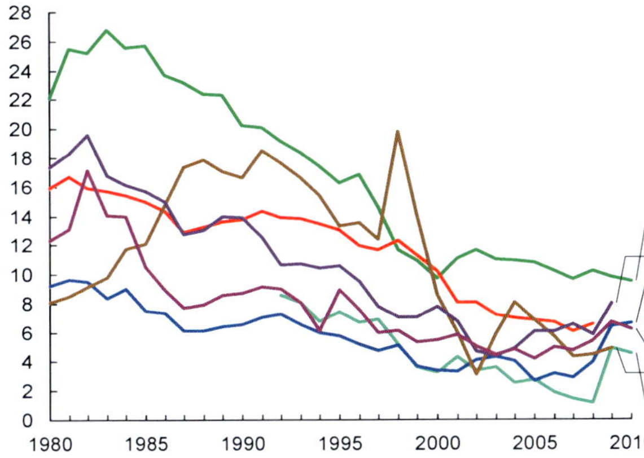

Change
Percentage points

	1980–90	1990–2000	2000–10
Italy	-1.9	-10.5	-0.2
Australia[1]	-3.4	-6.2	0.2
US	-2.7	-3.2	3.2
Japan[2]	-2.1	-3.5	-3.7
Canada	-3.6	-3.3	0.8
S. Korea[1]	8.6	-8.1	-3.7
UK	n/a	-5.3[3]	1.3

1 Data available through 2009.
2 Data available through 2008.
3 Covers 1992–2010.
SOURCE: McKinsey Insights China; McKinsey Global Economic Growth Database; National sources; McKinsey Global Institute

The increasing availability of credit is another factor that lowered household saving, particularly in countries such as the United Kingdom and the United States. This is because saving is defined as after-tax income less consumption, and increased borrowing boosts consumption.[31] In addition, easily available credit also lowers household saving because it reduces the need to save for large purchases such as a car or a down payment on a house. Indeed, differences in the accumulation of household debt are one factor explaining the differences in household saving between some mature economies, such as the United States and Germany.

Another factor causing household saving rates to fall in some countries was the "wealth effect" of asset appreciation during the 1990s stock market boom and the real estate bubbles that occurred in many countries after 2000. As households saw their stocks, homes, and other assets soar in value, they spent more and saved less than they otherwise would have. There is strong empirical evidence of this effect.

29 For example, see Bosworth and Chodorow-Reich, November 2006; or Farrell and Greenberg, May 2005.

30 *Talkin' 'bout my generation: The economic impact of aging US baby boomers*, McKinsey Global Institute, June 2008.

31 Mortgages raise household investment in housing and are not considered consumption.

In the United States, for example, consumption rises by about 5 cents for every $1 increase in household wealth.[32]

The impact of increased credit availability and the "wealth effect" on saving can be seen in the United States. US saving in retirement plans has declined since the 1980s, and nonretirement saving as a share of disposable income turned negative until 2008, when lending standards were tightened (Exhibit 11).[33] Many Americans saw their houses and stocks appreciate for such a long time that they felt little need to save much of their incomes.

Exhibit 11

From 1985 to 2007, US households saved less than their pension contributions, taking out debt to finance consumption

Components of US household saving, 1952–2009

% of disposable personal income

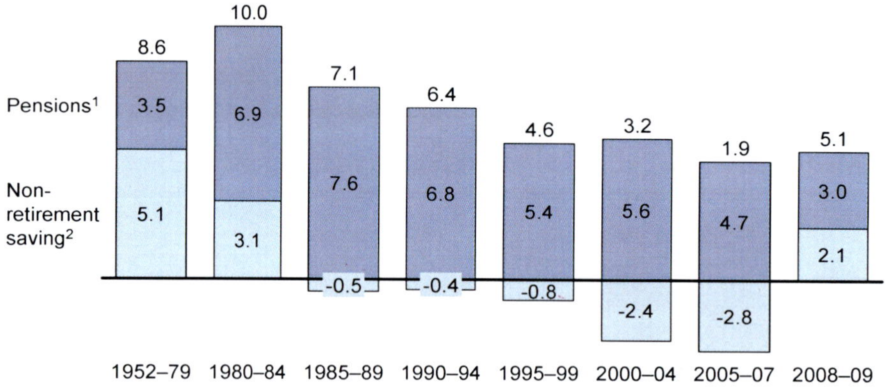

1 Includes public and private pension plans, 401(k) plans, and individual retirement accounts; does not include Social Security withholdings.

2 Other saving calculated through the change in household assets less liabilities, excluding retirement saving.

SOURCE: Bosworth & Bell (2005); US National Income and Product Account; US Federal Reserve Flow of Funds Accounts; McKinsey Global Institute

Corporate saving rose over the past three decades

Gross corporate saving[34] increased from 10 percent of GDP in 1980 to 13.3 percent in 2008 in the mature countries in our sample (Exhibit 12), and now accounts for around 70 percent of gross national saving, up from 54 percent in 1995. In some countries, such as Germany, Japan, and the United Kingdom, corporate saving now exceeds corporate investment, making companies net suppliers of capital to the rest of the economy. This is a reversal of the historical pattern, in which households were the net savers in the economy and companies borrowed from banks or through capital markets to finance their investment. As we write this report, there is much discussion about large and growing corporate cash balances, but they are different from savings (see sidebar: *Corporations' cash holdings and savings*).

32 See, for instance, Muellbauer, April, 2008; Feldstein, 2006; and *The Economic Report of the President*, February 2010.

33 See Bosworth and Bell, 2005, for a more detailed discussion of US household saving.

34 In economic terms, gross corporate saving comprises retained earnings (or undistributed profits) and the depreciation allowance of the firm's capital goods. This is the cash flow after dividends are paid but before investment. In developed countries, the depreciation allowance is the largest component of corporate saving, reflecting companies' large capital stock. See the technical appendix for more detail.

Exhibit 12

In developed countries, the household saving rate has declined while the corporate saving rate has increased

Household and corporate gross saving in developed countries,[1] 1980–2008

% of total GDP, nominal values

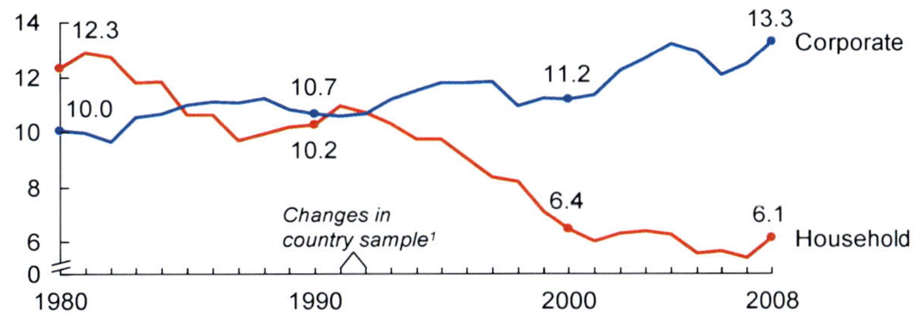

$ trillion	1980	1990	2000	2008
Total GDP	5.4	12.3	21.6	33.9
Household gross saving	0.7	1.3	1.4	2.1
Corporate gross saving	0.5	1.3	2.4	4.5

1 Based on a sample comprising Australia, Canada, France, Germany (from 1991 onward), Italy, Japan, South Korea, the United Kingdom (from 1992 onward), and the United States.

SOURCE: McKinsey Global Economic Growth Database; United Nations System of National Accounts; McKinsey Global Institute

Corporations' cash holdings and savings

Corporate cash holdings have increased by $1.9 trillion since 2000 in the major economies, reaching $3.8 trillion in 2009—some $800 billion higher than if they had grown at the same pace as GDP (Exhibit 13). Some policy makers are now calling for companies to invest this money to create jobs. However, corporate saving is not the same as these cash balances.

Exhibit 13

Corporate cash balances have increased by $1.9 trillion since 2000 in the major economies

Cash holding of publicly listed companies,[1] 2000 and 2009

% of GDP

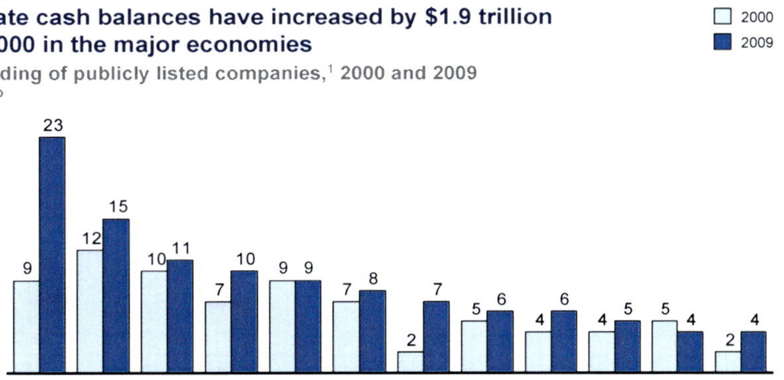

	South Korea	Japan	France	US	UK	Germany	Australia	China	Canada	Spain	Italy	Mexico
Increase in cash holdings $ billion	144	238	144	766	63	140	54	259	45	45	29	15

1 Cash holdings defined as cash and short-term investments.

SOURCE: McKinsey Corporate Performance Analysis Tool; McKinsey Global Institute

Companies can use their saving for investment, acquisitions, share repurchases, and paying down debt. The amount left over after such spending is the change in the cash balance.

There are several additional reasons that corporate cash balances are higher today than in the past. First, companies found during the crisis in 2008 that credit markets can freeze and cut off needed operational funding, prompting them to keep more cash on hand. Second, particularly for US companies, repatriating cash from foreign subsidiaries results in a tax liability. Moreover, some companies are waiting to invest or make acquisitions once aggregate demand increases and uncertainty clears about the strength of the economic recovery.

We see marked differences in corporate saving rate trends across countries (Exhibit 14). Rates rose the most in Asia, Canada, and the United Kingdom but fell in France, Italy, and Spain. The reasons reflect many different factors, including variations in the profitability of different sectors and their weight in the economy, tax treatment of corporate profits, depreciation allowances, and dividend payout practices.

Exhibit 14

Corporate saving rates increased most in Asian economies

Corporate saving rate in selected countries, 1998 and 2008

% of GDP, nominal values

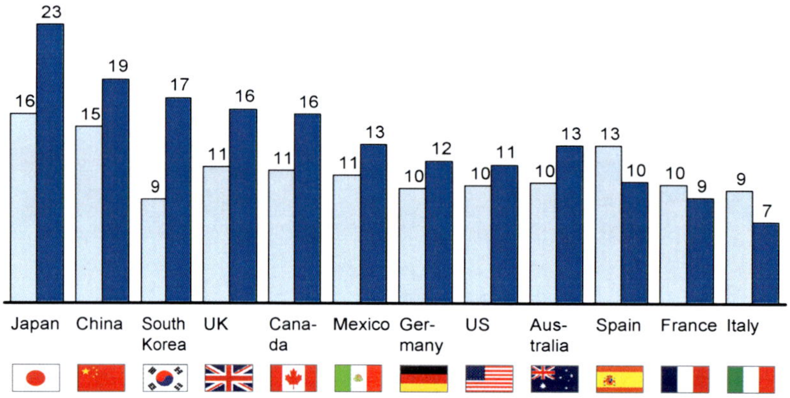

	Japan	China	South Korea	UK	Canada	Mexico	Germany	US	Australia	Spain	France	Italy
Increase in nominal saving $ billion	499	659	128	265	167	98	219	761	88	83	105	41

SOURCE: McKinsey Global Economic Growth Database; United Nations System of National Accounts; national sources; McKinsey Global Institute

In Japan, for example, the high gross corporate saving rate, despite relatively low profitability, is possible because of the strong cash flow from large depreciation allowances following several decades of heavy investment in capital assets. In China, the rise in the corporate saving rate reflects growth in profitability, low dividend payout ratios and relatively low corporate taxes. In the United Kingdom, much of the increase in corporate saving comes from rising profits in its financial sector, which accounted for a growing share of national GDP during the credit bubble years, and which, with the benefit of hindsight, might have been illusory.

In the United States, the increase in the corporate saving rate is the result of companies' growing use of share repurchases and an anomaly in the way these repurchases are accounted for. In the national accounts, gross corporate saving is defined as retained earnings (or profits) plus a depreciation allowance. When corporations pay dividends to shareholders, the amount is subtracted from profits to yield retained earnings and therefore lowers measured corporate saving. But if a company instead uses income to buy back shares, the amount is not subtracted from retained earnings, and thus does not lower saving. The recorded US corporate saving rate would have declined since the 1990s if companies compensated shareholders through dividends rather than share repurchases (Exhibit 15). This is an anomaly in the national accounts, as business executives today view dividends and share repurchases as alternative ways of returning profits to shareholders. In the United Kingdom, share repurchases would have offset more than a fifth of 2007 gross corporate saving if they instead had been paid out as dividends. However, share repurchases are not as common outside the United Kingdom and the United States, and so do not explain the rise of corporate saving in other countries.

Exhibit 15

Excluding share repurchases, the US corporate saving rate would have declined over the past 30 years

Private saving and share repurchases in the US, 1962–2008

% of GDP (3-year moving average)

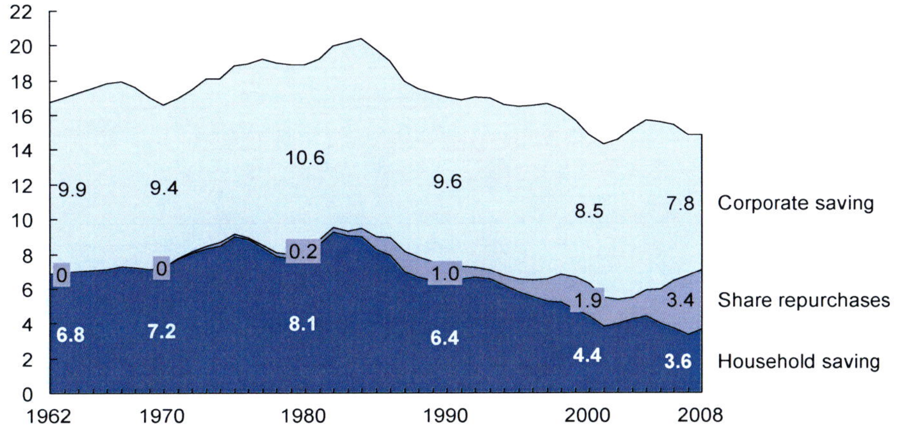

SOURCE: US Bureau of Economic Analysis; McKinsey Corporate Performance Analysis Tool; McKinsey Global Institute

Government saving closely tracks the business cycle

Government saving[35] accounts for just a small portion of the total saving in most countries in normal times. Over the past two business cycles, government saving averaged 1.1 percent of GDP in our sample of 14 countries. Moreover, it is highly cyclical, rising during economic expansions as tax revenue rises and public assistance spending falls. This process goes into reverse during recessions. Therefore, we see that the government saving rate rose in many countries during the dot-com boom of the late 1990s and during the credit bubble of the past decade. The rate fell sharply in 2009 (down 5.6 percentage points from 2008 levels), particularly in developed countries that enacted stimulus plans. When government budget deficits grow, it represents dissaving, and thus reduces gross national saving.

1.4 TRENDS IN NATIONAL SAVING AND INVESTMENT HAVE RESULTED IN GLOBAL IMBALANCES

Globally, realized saving and investment equal one another by definition. But in a world of open economies and global capital markets, surplus saving in one country can flow across borders to finance investment in another. Thus, at a national level,

35 Gross government saving is measured differently than the more commonly discussed fiscal balances. Saving is defined as the government's revenue minus consumption. The fiscal balance is revenue minus the sum of consumption and investment. Therefore, a government's fiscal balance is usually less than its gross government saving. See the technical appendix for more detail.

saving and investment do not have to be equal. Countries that save more than they invest, such as China, run current account surpluses, and thus are net capital exporters (net lenders) to the world as their excess saving is invested abroad. Countries that invest more than they save, such as the United States, run current account deficits, and thus are net capital importers (net borrowers). The divergent trends in saving and investment discussed above thus explain current account balances and the net capital flows between countries.[36]

Consider the United States. We saw earlier that, in contrast to other mature economies, the US investment rate has not declined but instead remained stable at around 20 percent of GDP. But the US household saving rate has fallen dramatically since 1980, reducing the overall national saving rate. This gap between US saving and investment has been funded by net capital inflows from foreign investors, equivalent to the current account deficit (Exhibit 16).

Exhibit 16

The US current account deficit from 2005 to 2009 absorbed all the surplus saving from China, the rest of Asia, and the Middle East

Cumulative current account balances, 2005–09

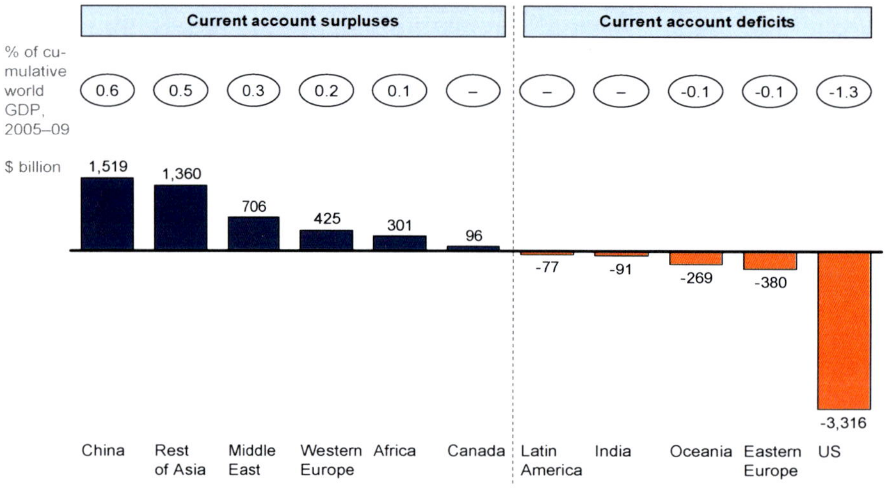

SOURCE: McKinsey Global Economic Growth Database; McKinsey Global Institute

The US current account deficit peaked at about 6 percent of GDP in 2006, or around $800 billion, and has declined since then to 3 percent in 2009. Policy makers seeking to reduce the current account deficit often focus on the trade balance. But an alternative approach would be to close the gap between saving and investment.

Germany presents a contrasting picture. Germany's investment rate has declined substantially since the 1970s, while its national saving rate has remained stable. The result is domestic saving that is higher than domestic investment, or a current account surplus. Even in 2009, the year of a global recession, Germany's current account surplus was equal to 5 percent of GDP, or around $170 billion.

Going forward, shifts in the level and pattern of global investment and saving will likely cause changes in interest rates and new patterns of net capital flows around the world.

36 This is a different way of defining current account deficits and surpluses from the more common definition, which is based on a country's trade balance. The two definitions are equivalent. See the technical appendix for more detail.

2. The coming global investment boom

The global investment rate began rising in 2002, primarily reflecting the surge in investment in China and India. In these countries and across other emerging markets, large rural populations are migrating to rapidly expanding cities, increasing the demand for new homes, public infrastructure, factories, transportation, offices, and shopping centers.[37] About 500 million more people live in cities today than did in 2002, and this growth is accelerating. Previous McKinsey Global Institute research estimated that the world's total number of urban residents will grow by 1.5 billion over the next two decades—more than the population of India today.[38] By 2030, China will have 44 urban areas with more than 4 million residents each, while India will have 11. This process will require trillions of dollars worth of investment, creating a burst of commercial opportunities for builders, engineers, developers, financiers, commodities suppliers, and others. And it has already begun.

The global investment rate rose from 20.8 percent of GDP in 2002 to 23.7 percent in 2008. Although global investment fell during the recession of 2009, figures from the first half of 2010 show it has picked up again.[39] If the current consensus forecast for GDP growth is realized, we project that global investment demand will reach about 25 percent of GDP[40] by 2030—a level not seen since the 1970s. This will mean investment of $24 trillion in 2030 at today's prices, or $13 trillion more than in 2008.

2.1 EMERGING MARKETS ARE INVESTING MORE

Business leaders and policy makers understand that capital investment can lay the foundation for long-term economic growth, increasing both profits and living standards. Investment is needed to create the factories and equipment that make goods, the roads and rail that help move goods, and the laboratories and schools that foster innovation. Strong growth expectations will spur strong demand for investment.

Rapid economic growth in emerging markets has therefore boosted their investment rates. China's investment rose to 43.9 percent of GDP in 2008, up from 35.0 percent in 1990. It rose even higher in 2009, to 49 percent of GDP, as the government increased public investment to stimulate the economy during the global recession (Exhibit 17). China is now investing at rates that surpass the peak rates of Japan (39.7 percent in 1970) and South Korea (39.9 percent in 1991). India's investment rate climbed to 39.5 percent of GDP in 2008, up from 23.5 percent in 2000.

---

37 Throughout this report, we define emerging markets as countries with average 2004-08 GDP per capita less than $14,500, excluding oil exporters. Mature economies are those with average GDP per capita at or above this threshold during this period, excluding oil exporters.

38 See Richard Dobbs, "Megacities," *Foreign Policy*, September/October 2010.

39 China has not released any investment data for 2010 as we write this report, and they will be a significant factor in determining the overall global investment rate.

40 We use nominal values for historical figures, but we hold prices and exchange rates constant at 2005 levels when projecting future rates. The consensus growth forecast is the average of those by the Economist Intelligence Unit, Global Insight, and Oxford Economics.

Other emerging markets are also investing more (Exhibit 18). Africa has boosted its investment rate to 24.1 percent of GDP in 2008 from 19.3 percent in 2000. Eastern Europe's rate rose to 26.4 percent from 21.4 percent over the same period. Investment in other emerging Asian countries remains strong as well.

Exhibit 17

Among emerging economies, investment rates in China and India have reached very high levels

Investment rate by country and year, 1970–2009

% of GDP, nominal values

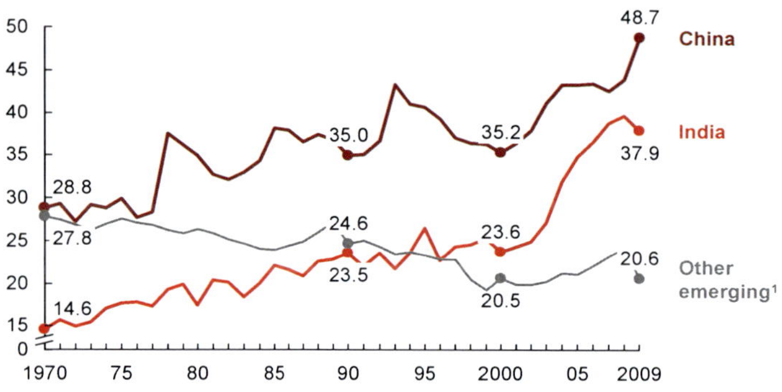

Change in rate
Percentage points

	1970–90	1990–2000	2000–09
China	6.2	0.2	13.5
India	8.9	0.1	14.3
Other emerging[1]	-3.2	-4.1	0.1

1 Countries with an average GDP per capita between 2004 and 2008 below $14,500, excluding China and India; 2009 data based on partial samples of 36 countries (equivalent to about 85 percent of GDP from emerging economies).

SOURCE: CEIC; Haver Analytics; McKinsey Global Economic Growth Database; World Development Indicators of the World Bank; McKinsey Global Institute

Exhibit 18

Investment rates have increased across all emerging market regions since 2000

Investment rate by region and year, 1970–2008

% of GDP, nominal values

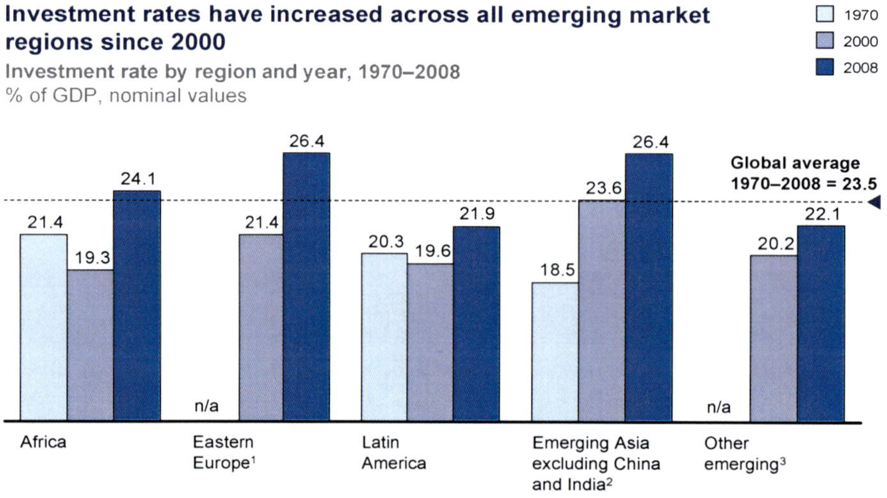

1 Bosnia and Herzegovina, Bulgaria, Croatia, Estonia, Hungary, Latvia, Lithuania, Poland, Romania, Russia, Serbia, Slovak Republic, and Ukraine.
2 Bangladesh, Malaysia, Philippines, Sri Lanka, Thailand, and Vietnam.
3 Armenia, Georgia, Jordan, Kyrgyz Republic, Mongolia, Pakistan, Turkey, Turkmenistan, and Uzbekistan.

SOURCE: McKinsey Global Economic Growth Database; World Development Indicators of the World Bank; McKinsey Global Institute

Oil exporters as a group have also invested more in absolute terms to take advantage of the near quadrupling of oil prices since 2002, to expand their infrastructure, and to diversify their economies. But they have not increased their overall investment rate. This is in part because their GDP has grown as oil prices have increased, therefore keeping the ratio of investment to GDP constant. But it is also because the rising investment rates of some oil exporters (such as those in the Gulf Cooperation Council)[41] have been offset by the falling rates of others (such as Russia and Norway).

Emerging markets are investing heavily in infrastructure and residential real estate

Today, São Paolo has more high-rise buildings than Tokyo, and the Brazilian city is adding more. In October 2010, China launched a high-speed rail line between Shanghai and Hangzhou to accommodate increased travel demand. And China plans to build new subway systems, highways, and high-speed trains in its top 170 cities.

This type of growth has turned infrastructure and home building into the fastest-growing categories of investment in emerging markets, surpassing growth in investment in factories and commercial buildings. Relative to GDP, developing economies invest more than twice as much as mature economies in infrastructure (5.7 percent versus 2.8 percent). The gap is seen in all categories of infrastructure but is particularly large in transportation (e.g., roads, airports, rail), followed by utilities (e.g., power and water systems) (Exhibit 19). In 2008 alone, China and India together spent more than $500 billion on new infrastructure, nearly as much as all of Western Europe and substantially more than the United States and Canada combined.

Exhibit 19

Infrastructure investment as a share of GDP is much higher in emerging markets than in developed economies

Investment in infrastructure as a share of GDP, 1980 and 2008

% of GDP, nominal values

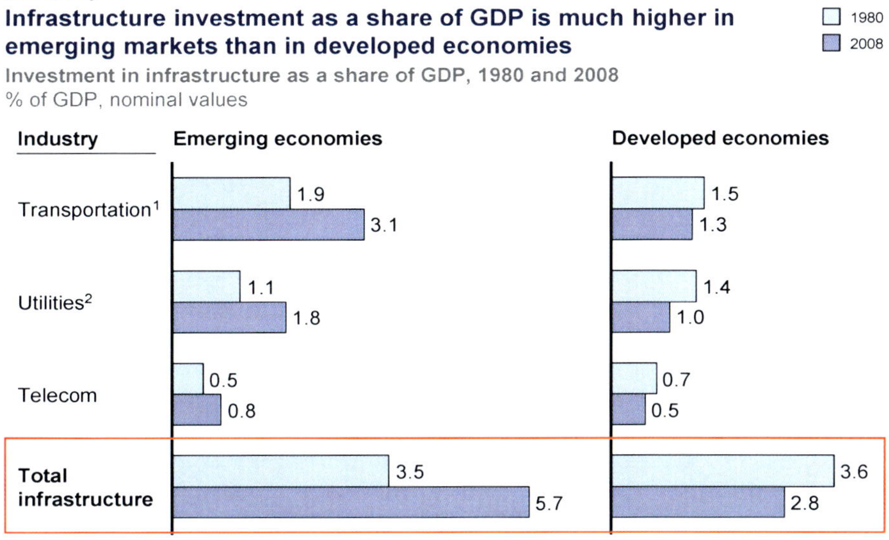

1 Includes land, road & rail transport, pipelines, water & air transport, post & courier delivery, and support transport activities.
2 Includes energy & gas supply, and water supply.
SOURCE: Global Insight; McKinsey Global Economic Growth Database; World Development Indicators of the World Bank; McKinsey Global Institute

Most developing countries currently invest less in residential real estate than mature economies as a share of GDP, reflecting their lower household income levels. India and Brazil currently invest just 1.6 percent of GDP in residential real estate, far below the mature market average of around 4.6 percent in 2008. But over time, this will change as incomes rise. China is already an exception because of its large, fast-growing urban population and expanding middle class. China invested 8.9 percent of GDP in housing in 2008, far above the recent US peak of 6.2 percent in 2005. Other

41 The Gulf Cooperation Council is a political and economic union of six states: Bahrain, Kuwait, Oman, Qatar, Saudi Arabia, and the United Arab Emirates.

developing countries will likely raise their investment rates in residential real estate in the decades to come, as more people move to cities and as their incomes rise.

Investment rates in China and India could remain high for decades

Earlier, we noted that China and India are investing at higher rates than did Japan and South Korea during their rapid periods of growth. In absolute terms, China already had built the third-largest stock of capital assets in the world by 2008, worth $8.2 trillion.[42] Relative to the size of its economy, these fixed assets were worth around 267 percent of China's GDP in 2008, a level similar to Germany's (at 264 percent) and higher than that of the United States (at 220 percent).

But when measured in per capita terms, the value of China's capital stock remains quite low compared with that of developed economies (Exhibit 20). The same remains true even if we measure the capital stock for just urban China: it amounts to about $6,200 per capita, compared with $55,000 in South Korea, $94,000 in the United States, and $136,000 in Japan. (Japan's very high level of capital stock per person partially reflects a decade of large public investment programs aimed at trying to revive economic growth.) These comparisons suggest that while China and India are investing at very high rates, they could continue to do so for many years to come, given the size of their needs.

Exhibit 20

Capital stock per capita in China and India is very low compared with that of developed countries

Capital stock vs. GDP per capita by country and year, 1980–2008

$ thousand, sample of selected countries, constant 2005 prices and exchange rates

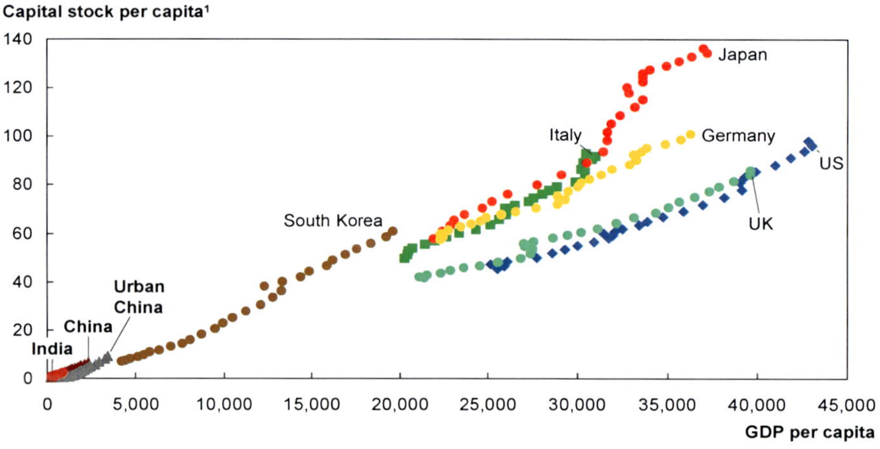

1 Stock of net fixed assets at the end of the year, assuming 5 percent depreciation rate for all the assets.

SOURCE: McKinsey Insights China; McKinsey Global Economic Growth Database; McKinsey Global Institute

Looking ahead, both China and India have vast investment requirements. Past McKinsey Global Institute research has found that, to keep pace with urban population growth, China would have to add 40 billion square meters of residential and commercial floor space by 2030, equivalent to adding one New York City every two years. And India would have to add between 800 million and 900 million square meters each year over the next two decades, equivalent to adding a Chicago each year, and would have to pave 2.5 billion square meters of roads, equivalent to 20 times

42 The stock of capital assets includes the value of all plants and buildings, equipment, machinery, infrastructure, and housing. It reflects the cumulative sum of annual investment, less depreciation. See the technical appendix for details on how we constructed capital stock figures.

the roads paved in the past decade.[43] Whether or not this level of investment will be realized—particularly in India—remains to be seen.

2.2 GLOBAL INVESTMENT COULD EXCEED 25 PERCENT OF GLOBAL GDP BY 2030 IF CURRENT GDP FORECASTS ARE REALIZED

As emerging markets continue to grow and urbanize, they are likely to drive the global investment rate higher. If the world economy recovers and current consensus GDP growth forecasts are met, we calculate that the annual investment in real terms will rise from 22.4 percent of global GDP in 2008 to 25.1 percent in 2030 (Exhibit 21)—an investment rate not seen since the 1970s.[44] This is a cumulative sum of about $30 trillion more investment between 2010 and 2030 than would have occurred if today's investment rate persisted. (For details on our model, see sidebar: *Methodology for investment projections*.)

Exhibit 21

In the consensus global growth scenario, global investment demand could increase to about 25 percent of GDP by 2030

Global investment rate, 1970–2030

% of global GDP

1 Based on actual prices and exchange rates of each year.
2 Shown in 2005 prices and exchange rates.
3 Forecast assumes the price of capital goods increases at the same rate as other goods and assumes no change in inventory.
SOURCE: Economist Intelligence Unit; Global Insight; McKinsey Global Economic Growth Database; Oxford Economics; MGI Capital Supply & Demand Model; World Bank's World Development Indicators; McKinsey Global Institute

In this scenario, global GDP is projected to grow at an annual rate of 3.2 percent from 2008 through 2030, higher than the 2.9 percent growth experienced from 1990 through 2008. This growth rate reflects the increasing GDP weight of rapidly growing emerging economies. Over the same period, many countries' working-age populations will grow more slowly. Reflecting these changes in demographics, US real GDP is projected to grow at an annual rate of 2.5 percent over the next two decades, Japan's at 0.7 percent, and Germany's at 1.2 percent. Meanwhile China's GDP grows at 7.7 percent and India's at 7.5 percent. In the next chapter, we consider different scenarios for GDP growth and their impact on both global investment and saving.

43 See *Preparing for China's urban billion*, McKinsey Global Institute, March 2009, and *India's urban awakening: Building inclusive cities, sustaining economic growth*, McKinsey Global Institute, April 2010.

44 We use nominal values for historical figures, but we hold prices and exchange rates constant at 2005 levels when projecting future rates. This allows us to compare 2030 amounts to today's investment. In the next chapter, we assess the impact of different exchange rate assumptions on our projection.

Methodology for investment projections

Our model of future investment is based on the Cobb-Douglas production function.[45] We project investment for productive assets (including plant and equipment, infrastructure, and commercial and industrial real estate) and for residential real estate separately, since residential real estate assets do not expand the productive capacity of an economy.

To project investment in productive assets, we use projections of real GDP and labor force growth rates as inputs to the model. As we will discuss later, we use the consensus forecast for global GDP growth in our first scenario. We assume that total factor productivity for most countries continues to grow at the same pace as in the past. The output of the model is the amount of investment needed to support the GDP growth. This model allows us to examine the sensitivity of the results to different GDP growth trajectories and productivity assumptions. To project investment in residential real estate, we assume that the ratio of residential housing assets to GDP in each country will continue to grow at the same rate as in the past, with a few exceptions. (For instance, we assume that the growth rate in the United States will be slower in the future because of the recent housing bubble.)

In the scenario described in this chapter, we take future GDP growth rates and labor force growth rates for each country as the average across three sources: The Economist Intelligence Unit, Global Insight, and Oxford Economics. In the next chapter, we consider different scenarios for GDP growth, including one that assumes a weak global recovery that lasts through 2015, and another that assumes a much slower growth rate for China and India through 2030.

45 See the technical appendix for more detail.

China and India account for most of the increase in the global investment rate

Almost all of the projected increase in global investment demand reflects the rising weight of China and India in the global economy. If current investment rates were maintained (and assuming no changes in exchange rates over the period), these two countries' increased share in global GDP alone would cause the global investment rate to rise to about 24.5 percent by 2030.

In our projection, China's investment rate declines slightly over the next two decades, from over 40 percent in 2008 before the crisis to 38 percent by 2030.[46] This is because China's future real GDP growth rate in the consensus forecast will be slower than in the past (7.7 percent for the next two decades, compared with 10.3 percent since 1990). One reason that China's investment rate does not decline even more is that its capital-output ratio, like that of other countries, continues to increase over time. Nonetheless, China's share of global investment more than doubles in this scenario, from about 12 percent in 2008 to 25 percent by 2030 (Exhibit 22). Its capital stock would be worth around $50 trillion in real terms in 2030, twice as much as Japan's and nearly as much as the US capital stock. In per capita terms, however, China's stock would continue to significantly lag behind that of the industrial economies, even if we consider only urban areas.

46 These figures differ from previously cited nominal investment rates because they reflect real investment and real GDP, as measured in constant 2005 prices and exchanges.

Exhibit 22

China's share of global investment will more than double in the next 20 years, reaching 25 percent of the total

CONSENSUS GLOBAL GROWTH SCENARIO

Global investment rate,[1] 2008–30

% of global GDP, constant 2005 prices and exchange rates

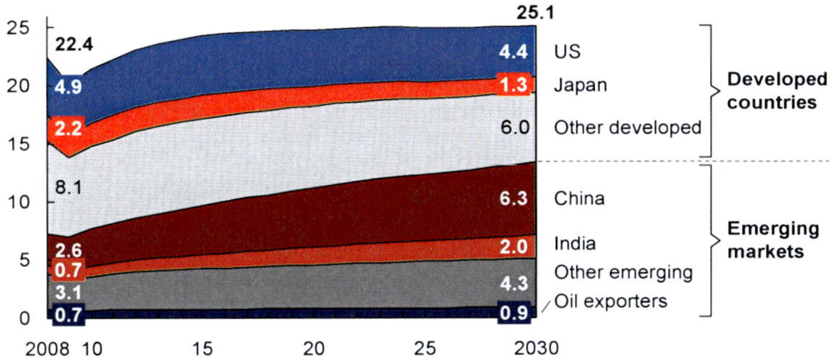

%	2008	10	15	20	25	2030
Developed countries' share	68	64	60	55	51	47
China's share	12	15	17	20	23	25

1 Forecast assumes the price of capital goods increases at same rate as other goods and assumes no change in inventory.
SOURCE: Economist Intelligence Unit; Global Insight; McKinsey Global Economic Growth Database; Oxford Economics; World Development Indicators of the World Bank; MGI Capital Supply & Demand Model; McKinsey Global Institute

We project that India's investment demand will rise over the next two decades, from about 35 percent in 2008 to 37.5 percent in 2030.[47] This increase is based on forecasts that India's economy continues to expand at about 7.5 percent per year—a higher rate than over the past 20 years—and that the country will invest heavily in infrastructure and residential real estate as its urban population grows. In particular, this scenario assumes that India's infrastructure investment will accelerate from 6.7 percent of GDP per year in 2008 to 7.5 percent (close to China's current investment rate in infrastructure) and that its investment in residential buildings will rise from 1.4 percent to 6.0 percent (still below the current 8.9 percent in China) over the next 20 years. In absolute terms, India's desired investment in infrastructure will total $380 billion in 2030 and its desired real estate investment will total $310 billion, about 40 percent and 20 percent of China's investment demand at that time, respectively.[48] This mainly reflects the smaller size of India's economy relative to China's, rather than differences in investment rates.

In this scenario, we also allow for an increase in infrastructure investment in the United Kingdom and United States. Both countries have invested in infrastructure at a slower pace than other developed economies since 1980: an average of 2.2 percent for the United States and 2.4 percent for the United Kingdom, compared with 3 percent for other developed countries. We assume that the US rate will rise to 2.6 percent by 2030 and that the United Kingdom rate will reach 3.2 percent.[49] Whether these increases are realized will depend upon fiscal constraints and a public commitment to renewing infrastructure. Even so, these increases may not be enough to achieve the complete renewal of these countries' aging and increasingly congested infrastructure.

47 These figures differ from previously cited nominal investment rates because they reflect real investment and GDP.

48 At constant 2005 prices and exchange rates.

49 The UK investment rate in infrastructure had already risen to 2.8 percent by 2008.

For example, 40 percent of London's water mains are more than 100 years old, and 12 percent are more than 150 years old.[50] The usage of the US public road system (measured in vehicle miles traveled) nearly doubled from 1980 to 2008, while capacity (measured in lane miles) increased by a total of just about 8 percent over the same period, causing congestion to increase sharply.[51] The American Society of Civil Engineers estimated that the United States needs to invest $1.2 trillion over a five-year period (worth about 1.5 percent of GDP per year) on top of current investment in transportation, water, energy, schools, waste disposal, and public parks and recreation in order to eliminate current deficiencies and expand capacity to meet growth in demand.[52] For the United Kingdom, similar estimates indicate a need to invest $140 billion over five years (worth about 1 percent of its annual GDP), in addition to current investment levels.[53]

In the consensus global growth scenario, investment demand in most other developed economies—including France, Germany, Italy, and Japan—is projected to decline slightly because of their slowing GDP growth and aging populations.

The mix of global investment will change

When mature economies invest, they are largely looking to "upgrade" their capital stock, replacing used capital goods with newer or higher-quality stock. Factories replace old machinery with more efficient equipment, and people make home improvements. But when emerging markets invest, they are starting from scratch, not upgrading or replacing old capital assets. They are constructing buildings, roads, and factories that will last for decades. So as emerging economies account for an expanding share of the global economy, their needs will drive growth in different types of investment.

As discussed earlier, emerging markets invest in infrastructure at more than twice the rate of mature economies. This makes sense, since many developing economies lack sufficient infrastructure and their cities are expanding rapidly. In addition, most developing countries' populations are growing faster and their household incomes are rising briskly, boosting demand for more and better housing. As we look forward over the next two decades, these two categories will account for greater shares of global investment.

- **Infrastructure:** In our consensus global growth scenario, infrastructure investment will rise from $1.6 trillion in 2008 to a desired level of about $3.7 trillion in 2030, as measured in constant exchange rates and prices (Exhibit 23). Whether this level is achieved will depend on whether global saving also increases. China will become the world's largest investor in both infrastructure and residential real estate (Exhibit 24). US and UK investment in infrastructure will also increase. In Japan, in contrast, investment in infrastructure is projected to decrease by 0.4 percentage points of GDP by 2030, falling from the very high rates of 1990 to 2009.

- **Residential real estate:** Historically, except during housing bubbles, housing investment as a share of GDP has increased very slowly in most countries. In absolute terms, however, global housing investment is projected to more than

---

50 HM Treasury of the United Kingdom, *National Infrastructure Plan 2010*.

51 The US Federal Highway Administration, 2008 highway statistics.

52 American Society of Civil Engineers, *2009 Report Card for America's Infrastructure*, 2009; and US Department of Transportation, *2006 Status of the Nation's Highways, Bridges, and Transit: Conditions & Performance*, 2006.

53 HM Treasury of the United Kingdom, *National Infrastructure Plan 2010*.

double over the next two decades, in a consensus global growth scenario, from $2.1 trillion in 2008 to a desired level of about $4.9 trillion in 2030. China and India together will account for almost 40 percent of the total in 2030, compared with 13 percent today.

- **Plant and equipment:** The remainder of the rise in global investment will be in commercial and other buildings, factories, and machinery and equipment. China, India, and the United States combined will account for about 70 percent of the growth in such investment over the next two decades.

Exhibit 23

In 2030, global desired residential real estate investment is expected to reach about $5 trillion per year, while desired infrastructure investment will reach about $4 trillion

CONSENSUS GLOBAL GROWTH SCENARIO

Desired global investment[1] by industry

$ trillion, selected years, constant 2005 prices and exchange rates

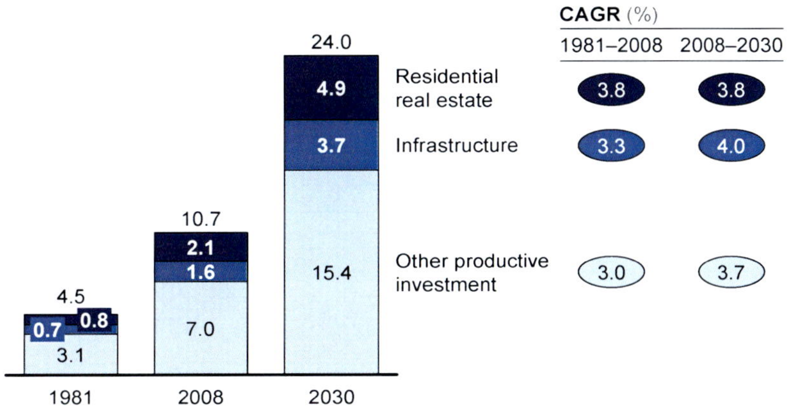

1 Forecast assumes the price of capital goods increases at same rate as other goods and assumes no change in inventory.

SOURCE: Economist Intelligence Unit; Global Insight; McKinsey Global Economic Growth Database; Oxford Economics; World Development Indicators of the World Bank; MGI Capital Supply & Demand Model; McKinsey Global Institute

Exhibit 24

China will be the largest investor in both infrastructure and residential real estate by 2030

CONSENSUS GLOBAL GROWTH SCENARIO

Selected countries, 2008 vs. 2030

$ billion, constant 2005 prices and exchange rates

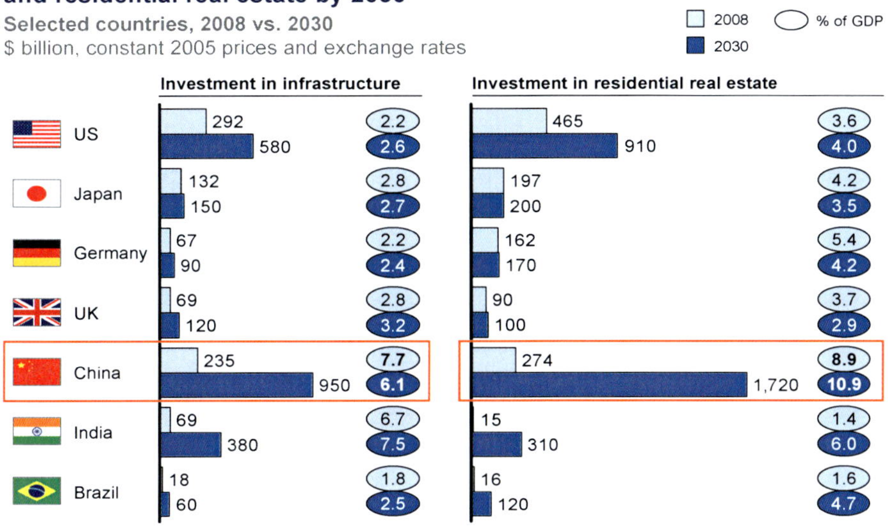

SOURCE: Economist Intelligence Unit; Global Insight; McKinsey Global Economic Growth Database; Oxford Economics; World Development Indicators of the World Bank; MGI Capital Supply & Demand Model; McKinsey Global Institute

2.3 CAPITAL PRODUCTIVITY, EXCHANGE RATES, AND ECONOMIC GROWTH COULD ALTER FUTURE DEMAND FOR INVESTMENT

Our projected investment demand of around 25 percent by 2030 is based on four critical assumptions: that the consensus forecast for global GDP growth is realized; that exchange rates do not change much; that the current rate of capital productivity growth continues; and that inflation in the prices of capital goods is the same as the inflation rate for the global economy. However, future investment demand could differ greatly from this projection if these assumptions are not realized.

In the next chapter, we examine how investment demand would be different in alternative scenarios for economic growth, and how it might be affected by changes in exchange rates, capital productivity, or the prices of capital goods relative to other goods. But before we turn to the discussion of investment scenarios, we will look at future saving.

3. Farewell to cheap capital

Rising investment demand will exert upward pressure on interest rates over the next 20 years if not matched by increased saving. From 2002 to 2008, the global saving rate increased from 20.5 percent of GDP to 24.0 percent because many of the developing countries with the highest rates—particularly China—accounted for an increasing share of the world's economy. But several trends, such as China's plans to boost its domestic consumption and the graying of the world's population, suggest that the world's saving rate may not increase much over the next two decades.

In this chapter, we look at how much the world would save in different scenarios for global GDP growth and exchange rates. Although saving must equal investment each year at the global level, we examine projections of the world's future saving separately from investment demand. Doing so allows us to examine the relative balance of supply of and demand for capital, and thus the direction and pressure on real interest rates (for detail, see technical appendix). Ultimately, real interest rates will adjust to bring global saving and investment into balance. In every scenario we consider except one, we find a substantial shortfall in desired saving relative to desired investment demand by 2030. This will likely raise long-term real interest rates, reducing realized investment and potentially dampening economic growth. If real rates return to their 40-year average, they would rise by 150 basis points; increased uncertainty about inflation could push real rates higher still.[54]

3.1 IN A CONSENSUS GLOBAL GROWTH SCENARIO, GLOBAL SAVING LAGS DESIRED INVESTMENT DEMAND BY $2.4 TRILLION IN 2030

As in our investment projections, we begin with consensus projections of GDP growth and hold prices and exchange rates constant. In this scenario, global GDP rises at 3.2 percent annually through 2030. In addition to these growth projections, we account for several structural shifts expected to affect global saving: a decline in China's saving rate as it increases consumption, a rise in the UK and US household saving rates as they replace lost wealth, and additional spending on pensions and health care for the elderly. Given these effects, we estimate that global desired saving will be around 22.6 percent of GDP in 2030—$2.4 trillion short of projected investment demand. This difference is an estimate made before interest rates adjust to bring actual investment and saving in line. We now look at the rationale for the key structural changes that determine our saving estimates.

China's saving rate will decline if its economy rebalances

In 2008, China overtook the United States as the largest saver in the world (Exhibit 25). Its government, households, and companies saved $2.3 trillion in

54 Long-term real interest rates are equal to the long-term nominal interest rate minus expected inflation over the life of the bond or loan. Real interest rates reflect the cost of borrowing, plus a risk premium to compensate investors for the possibility that inflation might increase more than expected. This risk premium could be rising today as central banks increase the money supply in an effort to spur more economic growth, creating greater investor uncertainty about future inflation.

nominal terms, equivalent to an astounding 53 percent of China's GDP. In doing so, China accounted for 23 percent of the global total, or almost one of every four dollars saved in the world that year. Chinese households and corporations have become the third- and fourth-largest sources of global saving in the world (Exhibit 26). In contrast, the national saving of Asia's other major saver, Japan, has declined dramatically (see sidebar: *Japan's saving ebbs*).

Exhibit 25

In 2008, China overtook the United States as the world's largest saver

Gross national saving

$ billion, nominal values

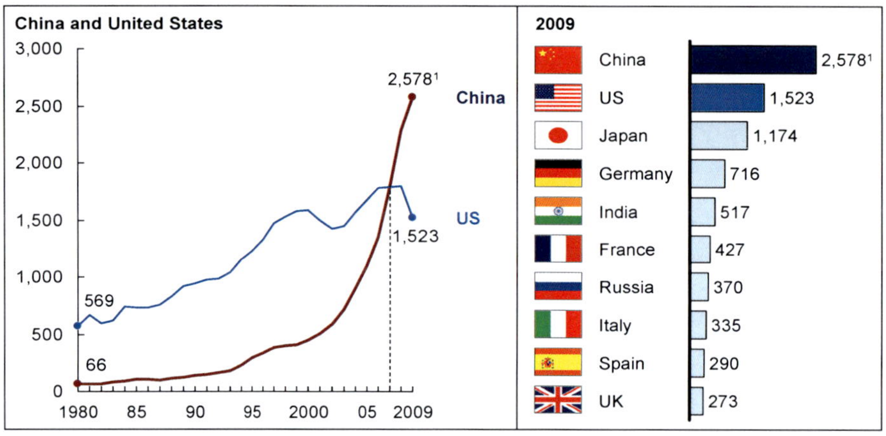

1 International Monetary Fund estimate (2009 figure).

SOURCE: CEIC; Haver Analytics; McKinsey Global Economic Growth Database; International Monetary Fund; World Development Indicators of the World Bank; United Nations System of National Accounts; McKinsey Global Institute

Exhibit 26

US and Japanese corporations are the largest pools of saving in the world, followed by Chinese households and corporations

Top ten gross saving sectors across countries, 1992 and 2008

Percent of total GDP,[1] nominal values

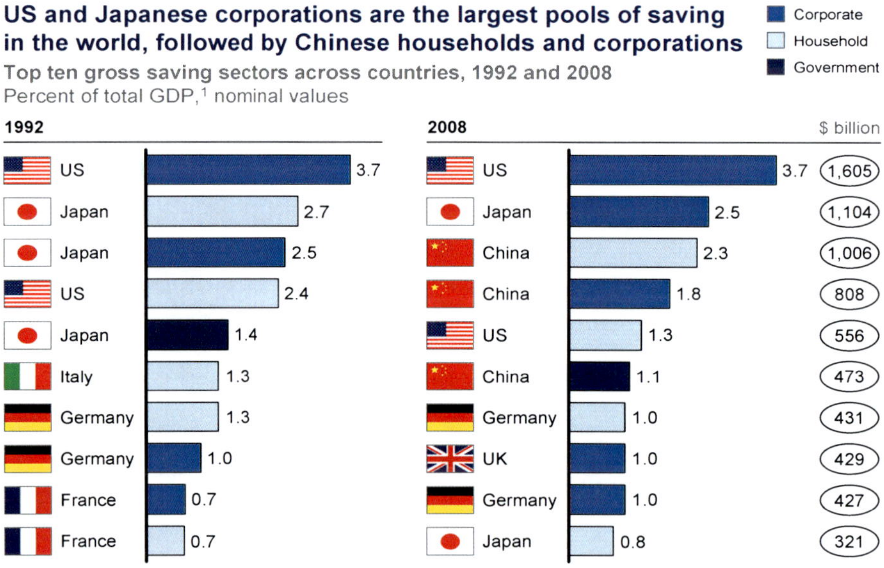

1 Australia, Brazil, Canada, China, France, Germany, India, Italy, Japan, Mexico, South Korea, Spain, the UK, and the US.

SOURCE: McKinsey Global Economic Growth Database; National sources; United Nations System of National Accounts; McKinsey Global Institute

Japan's saving ebbs

Japan is the world's third-largest saver, after the United States and China. However, Japan is not the super saver it once was. The country's saving rate has fallen dramatically, primarily because of the sharp decline in household saving as its population has aged. Japan's gross national saving fell from a recent peak of 34.8 percent of GDP in 1991 to 28.6 percent in 2008—a drop of more than 6 percentage points. The country remains a large net saver because its investment rate has fallen as well, by about 13 percentage points over the same period—creating a domestic version of the "saving glut."

Japan's household saving fell from 16 percent of GDP in 1980 to just 6.5 percent in 2008. This is due mainly to the impact of aging. As the population ages, a shrinking share of the population is of working age, while an increasing portion is retired and either earning less or drawing down their assets. Japan's government has also lowered the national saving rate by borrowing heavily during the past two decades in efforts to revive the economy. Gross government saving fell from a peak of about 8 percent in 1990 to about minus 3 percent in 2004 and is now around zero. Japanese corporations, meanwhile, have partially offset the decline in household and government saving. Corporate saving rose significantly over the past two decades, to more than 22 percent of GDP in 2008, more than three times as high as the household rate.

All sectors of China's economy—households, corporations, and the government—save at very high rates. Household saving was equal to 23 percent of GDP in 2008, one of the highest rates in the world. China's corporate saving rate has grown faster than household saving, reflecting strong productivity gains, low corporate taxes, and low dividend payouts. China's government gross saving has grown rapidly as well, reflecting robust growth in tax receipts and public investment.

However, if China follows the historical experience of other countries, its saving rate will decline over time as the country grows richer, as occurred in Japan and South Korea (Exhibit 27). It is unclear when this process will begin. But already, the country's leaders have started to craft policies that will reduce saving in order to rebalance its economy.[55] One goal will be to increase household income growth, which will raise household consumption as a share of GDP, reversing the decline of the past five years. China's rising wages are a step in this direction.

The government has plans to increase public programs for health care and pensions as well, which would give Chinese households less reason to save for precautionary reasons. Taiwan's saving fell after the government enacted such measures in 1995. Its household saving rate declined by about 7 percentage points of household income from 1995 to 2008 due to both those policies as well as other factors. If China experienced a similar decline due to such public programs, its household saving as a share of GDP would decline from 23 percent to about 17.5 percent.

55 Plans to increase consumption, and hence reduce saving, are being incorporated into the 12th Five-Year Plan. For potential policy changes, see *If you've got it, spend it: Unleashing the Chinese consumer*, McKinsey Global Institute, August 2009; Guonan Ma and Wang Yi, 2010.

Exhibit 27

Household saving rates in China and India are very high, but the experience of more developed countries suggests they will eventually decline

Household saving rate vs. GDP per capita, 1960–2008

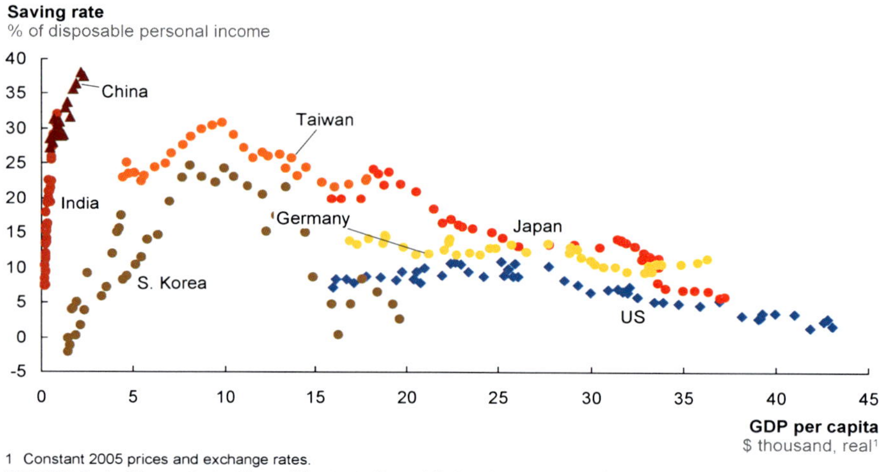

1 Constant 2005 prices and exchange rates.

SOURCE: Bank of Japan, Bank of Korea; Directorate-General Budget Accounting and Statistics, Republic of China; Global Insight; McKinsey Insights China; McKinsey Global Economic Growth Database; Reserve Bank of India; US Bureau of Economic Analysis; World Development Indicators of the World Bank; McKinsey Global Institute

Other factors may also reduce Chinese household saving in the years ahead. One is China's aging population. As workers retire, they begin drawing down the savings they accumulated in their working years. This could lower China's household saving rate. Another factor is the increasing availability of consumer credit and insurance. Although very small today, these markets are growing rapidly. Both credit and insurance enable households to respond to emergency events in ways other than saving, and so could boost consumption. Considering these factors, some external analysts forecast that China's household saving rate will fall by half or more over the next two decades, to Germany's level of around 10 percent of GDP.

China's corporate saving rate may also decline over time as the economy becomes more open to global competition, which would reduce profit margins, and as the very rapid productivity gains of the past slow. Companies also would have a lower saving rate if they had to pay higher wages and corporate taxes and pay out more dividends. However, if companies paid more in dividends, the recipients—the government and households—might save more. All together, these changes would lower China's corporate saving rate from its current 19 percent of GDP, which is far above the 10 to 12 percent average in mature economies and above China's own long-term average corporate saving rate of 15.5 percent.

The shifts outlined previously could lower China's saving rate from 52.5 percent of GDP to around 41 percent of GDP.[56] Combined with our investment projections for China, this would reduce the current account surplus to 3 percent of GDP by 2030, achieving the country's policy goal of rebalancing the economy. But globally, less saving in China may create shortfalls elsewhere, as it reduces global saving by around 2 percentage points.

56 This assumes that China's household saving rate declines from 22.5 percent in 2007 to 18 percent in 2030, the government's saving rate falls from 11 percent to 5 percent over the same period, and the corporate rate decreases from 19 percent to 18 percent.

US and UK households may increase their saving because of their loss of wealth

The 2008 financial crisis wiped out trillions of dollars in households' perceived wealth in the mature economies. In the United States, for instance, households lost $11 trillion through the fall in home equity and financial asset prices between mid-2008 and mid-2010.[57] Credit also tightened sharply, reducing consumers' ability to borrow. Consumer spending dropped sharply as well. As a result, the US household gross saving rate more than doubled from 2.8 percent of GDP in the third quarter of 2005 to 6.6 percent in the second quarter of 2010 (Exhibit 28). Some projections suggest US households will continue to save at around this rate or even higher for years to come.[58]

Part of this increase in saving reflects the desire to replace lost wealth—the "wealth effect" in reverse. But in addition, many Americans had not saved sufficiently for their retirement even before the crisis.[59]

Exhibit 28

The US household saving rate has declined since 1980, but has risen substantially since the start of the financial crisis

US gross household saving, January 1980–June 2010

% of GDP

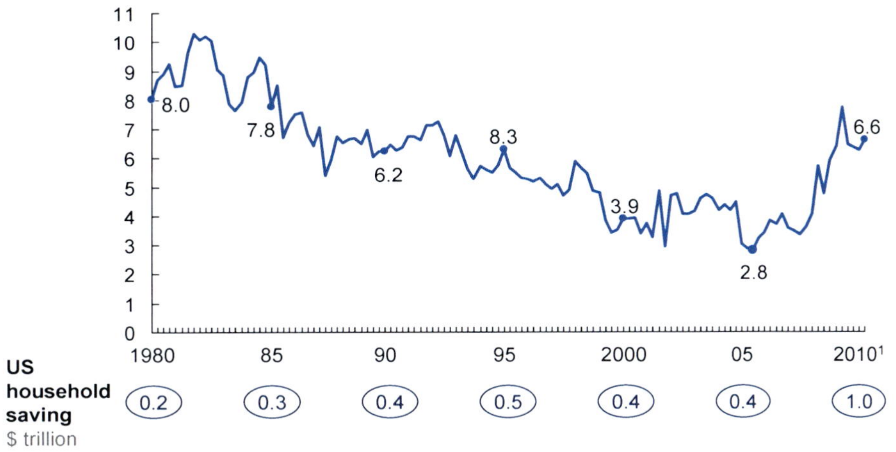

1 June 2010.

SOURCE: Bureau of Economic Analysis; McKinsey Global Institute

UK households are in a similar situation. Their gross saving rate as a share of GDP fell from 8.6 percent in 1992 to 1.4 percent in 2007, as both consumer credit availability and household assets increased. By mid-2010, UK households had recovered much of the wealth they lost because of the crisis. Still, the impact of the crisis on their saving rate has been substantial. As a share of GDP, UK household saving more than tripled from 1.4 percent in 2007 to 4.5 percent in the first six months of 2010.

57 See *Will US consumer debt reduction cripple the recovery?*, McKinsey Global Institute, March 2009.

58 See *The Economic Report of the President*, 2010.

59 Previous MGI research found that about two-thirds of US households headed by Americans born in the first decade of the baby boom (1945–54) had not saved enough to maintain their lifestyle in retirement. See *Talkin' 'bout my generation: The economic impact of aging US baby boomers*, McKinsey Global Institute, June 2008.

Going forward, we assume that UK and US households continue to save at their 2010 rates. That would raise the global saving rate by 1 percentage point and partially offset the decline in saving that will occur as China increases its consumption.

Governments will spend more to care for aging populations

The current financial crisis and recession led to a sharp increase in fiscal deficits across mature economies, turning their governments' gross saving rates negative. In the United States and United Kingdom, such government dissaving offset 39 percent and 32 percent, respectively, of all private saving in 2009 (Exhibit 29). However, a recent study by the International Monetary Fund (IMF) estimates that 70 percent of the change in fiscal positions was due to the drop in government tax revenue and the increase in public assistance spending driven by the recession.[60] A robust economic recovery will therefore close a substantial part of these deficits automatically, as will planned government cost-reduction programs. But a longer-term budget challenge looms: aging populations.

Exhibit 29

In 2009, government dissaving in the US and the UK offset 39 percent and 32 percent, respectively, of all private saving

Decomposition of total gross saving rate per economic sector in selected countries, 2009

% of GDP, nominal values

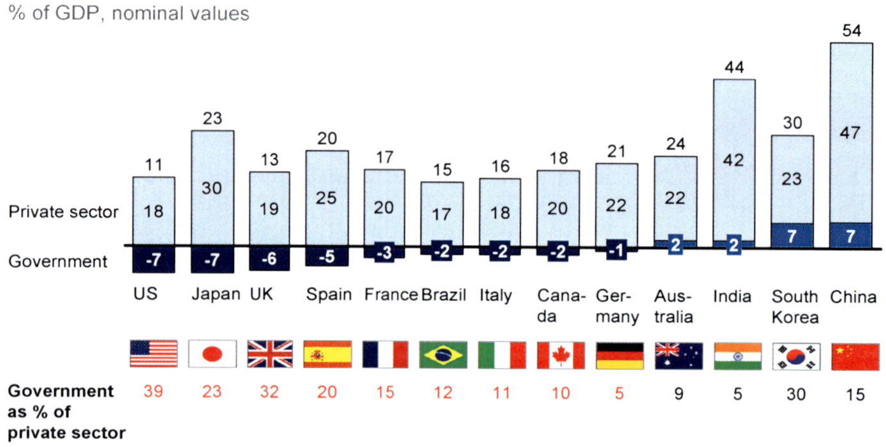

NOTE: Some figures do not sum due to rounding.
SOURCE: Haver Analytics; International Monetary Fund; Global Insight; McKinsey Global Institute

By 2030, the portion of the population over age 60 will reach record levels around the world. This will be particularly challenging in the mature economies. In Japan, 37 percent of the population will be over age 60, a 7 percentage point increase from 2010. In South Korea, the increase is even more dramatic, from 16 percent in 2010 to 32 percent in 2030. In the United States, 25 percent of the population will be 60 or older by 2030, while in Germany and Italy, the figure will reach 36 percent. Many emerging economies also will be challenged: the proportion of elderly in China will reach 25 percent over the same time period.

In mature countries, most people in retirement receive some form of government pension, as well as publicly provided health care, long-term care, and other benefits. The cost of providing these services will rise along with the growing ranks of elderly. We rely on several recent forecasts to determine the scale of additional age-related spending by 2030. The IMF projects an increase in spending of 3.6 percentage

60 International Monetary Fund, Fiscal Monitor (May 2010).

points of GDP for its sample of G-20 countries, which assumes a number of planned reforms to limit growth in government debt. Standard & Poor's uses a larger sample of countries and forecasts an average 3.4 percentage points of GDP increase in age-related spending (Exhibit 30). The Center for Strategic and International Studies provides a gloomier outlook, projecting an increase of 6.2 percentage points of GDP, assuming few changes to current policies.

Exhibit 30

By 2030, aging will cause governments around the world to spend more on health care and pensions

Range of increase in age-related public spending, 2010–30

Percentage points of country GDP

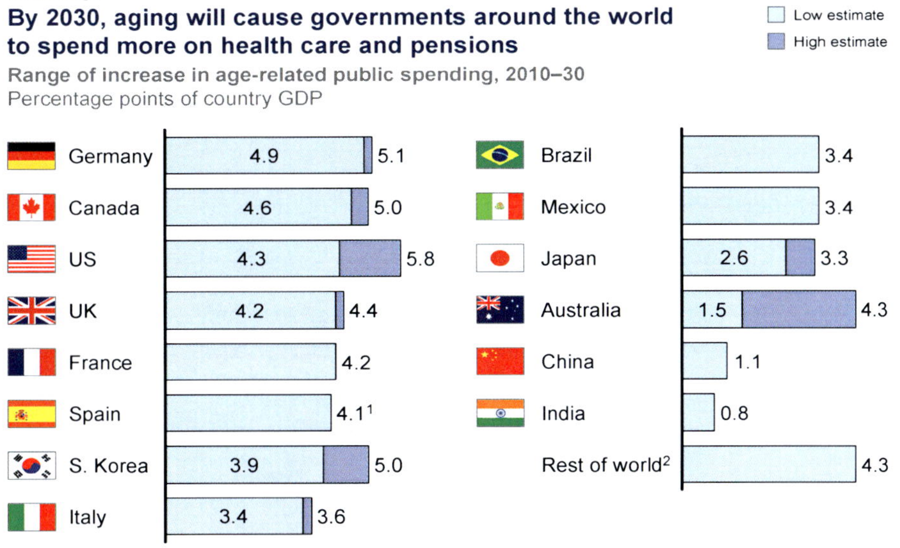

1 International Monetary Fund projection not available.
2 27 additional countries from Standard & Poor's, including both developed and emerging.
SOURCE: Standard & Poor's; International Monetary Fund Fiscal Monitor (May 2010); McKinsey Global Institute

Of course, governments can reduce the impact on their budgets of age-related spending by raising taxes, extending the retirement age, cutting benefits in other ways, or increasing pension contributions rates. But this may have the effect of reducing household and corporate saving. So one way or another, age-related spending is likely to lower saving. Using Standard and Poor's estimate, this increase in age-related spending would reduce global saving by 3.4 percent of GDP by 2030—a potentially far larger effect than the rebalancing of China's economy.

The $2.4 trillion gap between global saving and desired investment in 2030

Putting together all these pieces, we see that in a scenario based on the consensus global growth forecast, global saving would amount to 22.6 percent of global GDP in 2030—significantly short of projected investment demand. This would put upward pressure on global interest rates, which in turn would bring global saving and investment into balance. It is unclear how much of the adjustment would come through lower investment as opposed to higher saving. If the entire adjustment came through lower investment, we calculate it would reduce the global economic growth rate, compared with that in the consensus forecast, by a little less than than 1 percentage point of global GDP per year. To avoid this outcome, it will be necessary to increase global saving or raise capital productivity.

Of course, other scenarios for economic growth and other structural factors could change the size of the gap between the world's willingness to save and its desired investment demand. We consider several other scenarios below.

3.2 ALTERNATIVE SCENARIOS ALSO LEAD TO A GAP BETWEEN DESIRED SAVING AND INVESTMENT DEMAND

It is possible that the consensus economic growth forecasts are too optimistic, so we consider additional scenarios in which global GDP grows more slowly. (See the technical appendix for more details on these scenarios.) We also consider the impact of the appreciation of emerging market currencies relative to mature country currencies. We still find, in each of these scenarios, that investment demand is likely to substantially exceed saving over the coming two decades, putting upward pressure on interest rates. However, the size of the gap varies in different scenarios (Exhibit 31).

Exhibit 31

All considered scenarios lead to a gap between saving and investment demand, which would put upward pressure on interest rates

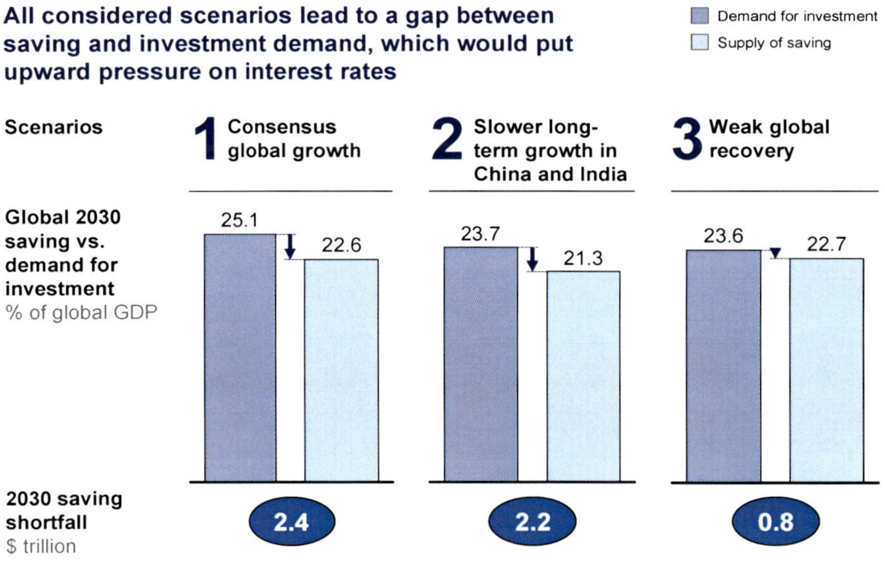

SOURCE: Economist Intelligence Unit; Global Insight; McKinsey Global Economic Growth Database; Oxford Economics; World Development Indicators of the World Bank; MGI Capital Supply & Demand Model; McKinsey Global Institute

As we discussed in Chapter 1, there is a strong link between economic growth and investment demand. Thus, if the global economy expands more slowly than in the consensus forecast, investment demand would rise more slowly as well. One scenario we consider is that in which China's and India's economies grow at much slower rates than in the consensus forecast (6 percent annual growth rather than 7.7 percent and 7.5 percent, respectively). In this scenario, we find that their investment demand would rise more slowly and their weight in the global economy would be less in 2030, both of which reduce the global investment rate. However, global saving would also be lower than in the consensus growth scenario. This is because the savings of China and India would account for a smaller share of the global savings pool in 2030. Additionally, China's corporate profits would likely be lower in a scenario of slower growth, and therefore the corporate saving rate would decline. Tax revenue would grow more slowly as well, possibly trimming China's very high rate of government saving and investment. Under these assumptions, we find that the global saving rate would still fall short of desired global investment demand, although there would be a smaller gap between the two than in the consensus growth scenario. Another scenario we consider, in which global GDP growth is very low until 2015, still results in lower willingness to save than desire to invest in 2030.

Only in the case of very slow global growth over the next two decades do we project that investment demand would fall enough to match the supply of saving. For this to happen, the global economy would expand at a compound annual rate of about 2.4 percent over the next two decades, well below the 3.2 percent annual rate in the consensus forecast. This could happen if economic growth rates in Brazil, China, India, and Mexico were to fall by about a quarter, and if growth rates in Japan, Europe, and the United States fell by about half, to 1.5 percent or lower. In such a case, the United States and European economies follow a path similar to that of Japan over the past two decades. In this case, we project that global investment demand would reach just 22.7 percent in 2030, roughly the same rate as saving.

Finally, we consider the impact of exchange rate changes over time. We do not predict how they will change, but we explored how our projections in the consensus global growth scenario might be altered by the real appreciation of emerging market currencies. Market opinion, economic theory, and historical experience all suggest that emerging markets' currencies will appreciate relative to mature country currencies as their economies grow and levels of income and wealth rise. Research has found that emerging market currencies tend to appreciate relative to the US dollar in real terms over time.[61] This currency appreciation effect increases the weight of emerging markets in the global economy by 2030 relative to mature countries. If this were to happen, we find that global investment demand would still exceed the supply of saving in 2030. The difference between the two would be larger in dollar terms than in the consensus forecast scenario, but would be the same as a share of global GDP, since both saving and investment in emerging markets would be worth more.

We did not consider how an appreciation of emerging market currencies would affect saving and investment rates in those countries. The effects of a stronger currency on both saving and investment are unclear. In China, for instance, consumers would pay relatively less for the goods they import from developed economies, which might increase household consumption and reduce saving. However, lower prices could instead enable families to purchase the same goods for less and thus save more. For Chinese companies, cheaper imported goods might mean they invest less in local currency terms, lowering their investment rate. Meanwhile, developed economies would pay more for the goods they import from emerging markets, which might dampen their consumption. The magnitude of the changes would depend on the price elasticity of imported consumer goods and capital goods in each country. We also did not consider the potential effects on saving and investment of a sharp rise in commodity prices, since that would merely transfer saving from the commodity consumers to the commodity producers, without a significant net change globally.

Another factor we considered is the effect on global investment of efforts to combat climate change. This could come through investments to bring greenhouse gas emissions to sustainable levels, or new investment required to adapt to the effects of global warming (for instance, increased investment in coastal defenses to address rising sea levels). Such investments would increase total global investment demand, and put additional upward pressure on interest rates (see sidebar: *Combating climate change could increase investment demand*).

---

61 This is known as the Balassa-Samuelson effect. See Bela Balassa, 1964; *Banque de France Bulletin Digest*, February 2004; and Samuelson, 1964.

Combating climate change could increase investment demand

Policy makers and business leaders are considering proposals to bring greenhouse gas emissions to sustainable levels, and to help people adapt to the effects of global warming. While there is still substantial uncertainty about the likely size of these investments, such measures are likely to increase investment demand, and also increase the gap between desired investment and saving, possibly putting additional upward pressure on real interest rates.

McKinsey analysis found that existing technologies could reduce carbon emissions by nearly 60 percent from 2005 levels—or 70 percent less than emissions would be if current trends persisted.[62] To meet these goals in 2030, for instance, 40 percent of new cars would have to be hybrids, 65 percent of electricity would have to be generated from low-carbon sources, and the world would have to avoid deforestation of an area twice the size of Venezuela. To realize the potential, investment in greenhouse gas abatement measures could rise by up to $485 billion per year through 2015 and rise further to as much as $1.3 trillion per year until 2030. Not all of this will be in addition to other projections of investment demand because some might occur as part of the normal replacement cycle. For instance, when cars reach the end of their useful life, they might be replaced by hybrids. And the required investment might be less due to technological innovation.

Additional investment will also be necessary to help populations adapt to the effects of climate change. Such investment could include building coastal defenses to address rising sea levels or forestry programs to fight desertification. The estimates of the annual costs of such efforts vary widely, from less than $50 billion annually to more than $150 billion.[63] It is unclear, however, what portion of these costs would be investment.

We therefore estimate that the annual additional incremental investment in 2030 could be up as much as $1 trillion. This would translate into increased global investment demand of around 1 percent of global GDP per year by 2030. In this case, the gap between the supply of saving and the demand for investment would grow larger than in our consensus growth scenario, creating more upward pressure on interest rates. And if saving does not rise enough to meet this higher investment demand, GDP growth would slow.

---

62 *Pathways to a low-carbon economy*; Version 2 of the global greenhouse gas abatement cost curve, McKinsey & Company, 2007.

63 See Agrawal and Fankhauser (2008), Parry, Arnell et al (2009), or World Bank (2010).

3.3 HIGHER REAL INTEREST RATES AHEAD

Interest rates today remain at 30-year lows, with little room to fall further. Borrowers should take advantage of these low rates while they can, because our analysis suggests that capital costs could start rising as the global economy recovers from the 2009 recession and as increasing investment demand outstrips savings. We cannot predict by how much interest rates may increase, nor predict the exact timing. But we can examine how they have moved in the past and look at the factors that may push them higher. We find that if real long-term interest rates were to return to their average since the early 1970s, they would rise by about 150 basis points. And this is not an issue for the distant future: real long-term rates may start moving up within five years as markets price in rapidly expanding investment demand.

If real rates were to return to their average over the past four decades, they would rise by 150 basis points

Real interest rates are a function of the supply of and demand for capital, and investor risk aversion. Predicting future levels of interest rates is therefore difficult and prone to error. To get a sense of how much interest rates could increase in the coming decades, we therefore instead analyzed how much rates would rise if they merely return to their historical averages (although there would be substantial differences between future economic conditions and any period in history). We looked at rates in the United States because it has had the largest and most liquid bond market in the world for some time. We found that real yields on US government bonds have varied widely since 1870 (Exhibit 32).

Exhibit 32

Real US interest rates would rise by 150 basis points if they returned to their 40-year average

Historic interest rates in the United States

Average yield to redemption on 10-year government bonds, 1870–2009, %

Time period	Real ex-post interest rates[1]	Nominal interest rates
Second Industrial Revolution and Gold Standard 1870–1913	3.2	3.7
WW I & II and interwar years 1914–45	1.4	3.4
Bretton Woods System 1946–71	0.5	3.9
Oil crises and inflation 1972–86	3.5	9.4
Beginning of the Great Moderation 1987-1999	4.3	7.1
Dot-com crash and recovery 2000–07	2.5	4.7
Global recession 2008–09	1.7	3.5

Average real ex-post interest rates[1]

Last 140 years (1870–2009) **2.3%**

Post-Bretton Woods System era (1972–2009) **3.3%**

1 Calculated as: nominal yield on 10-year bonds in current year, minus average realized inflation over next 10 years. To calculate 2001–09, we use Organisation for Economic Co-Operation and Development estimates of inflation in 2009–19.

SOURCE: Ferguson (2008); MeasuringWorth; International Monetary Fund International Financial Statistics; Organisation for Economic Co-Operation and Development; McKinsey Global Institute

The 140-year average real interest rate for the United States is 2.3 percent. Since the early 1970s, when financial liberalization enabled the emergence of global capital markets, the average US real interest rate has been considerably higher, at 3.3 percent. Thus, if US real interest rates were to return to their 140-year average, the real yield on the 10-year Treasury bond would rise by 50 basis points to 2.3 percent. If the yield returned to its average since the early 1970s, it would increase by 150 basis points to 3.3 percent. A similar increase could be seen if rates during the imminent emerging markets' investment boom returned to those that occurred during the US industrial revolution, another period of high investment demand. In this case, interest rates could rise by 140 basis points to 3.2 percent.

Moreover, these estimates of potential interest rate increases may be on the low side if investment demand is relatively inelastic. Many corporate executives report that interest rates are just one factor that influences the size and timing of investment decisions. Other factors include the overall economic outlook, the company's strategy, and the competitive environment.

We find that the growing imbalance between the world's saving rate and desired investment will be significant by 2020. However, long-term rates—such as the yield on a 10-year bond—could start rising even within the next five years as investors anticipate this future structural shift. Furthermore, the move upward is unlikely to be a onetime adjustment, since the projected gap between the demand for and supply of capital widens continuously from 2020 through 2030.

Other economic forces could put additional upward pressure on long-term rates

Although central bank monetary policy greatly influences short-term interest rates, economists debate whether monetary policy affects real long-term rates in ways beyond its impact on inflation expectations.[64] Real interest rates reflect the cost of capital, as determined by capital supply and demand, plus a risk premium to compensate investors for the possibility that inflation may rise more than expected.

In the United States during the 1970s, the combination of oil shocks and easy monetary policy in response to recessions made inflation rise much higher than had been expected, causing real interest rates to fall into negative territory. Subsequently, however, real ex-post interest rates soared to historic highs, because investors anticipated higher inflation than occurred and they demanded a large premium for the risk of unexpected future inflation.[65] Since the Federal Reserve conquered inflation in the early 1980s, inflation expectations have fallen steadily—though it took nearly 20 years to quell investors' fears of unexpected inflation. Indeed, in the developed world, confidence in central banks' abilities to keep inflation at stable levels has not only reduced nominal interest rates, but may also have contributed to the decline in real interest rates, as the inflation risk premium ebbed. Today, many investors anticipate higher inflation ahead, as indicated by the markets for inflation-linked bonds. If the credibility of central banks' monetary policies declines, there is a risk of additional upward pressure on both real and nominal interest rates.

At the same time, the nominal yield curve for conventional US Treasuries has steepened dramatically since 2007. The difference in yields for one-year notes and 10-year bonds was just 0.1 percentage points in 2007; by 2009, the difference had widened to 2.8 percentage points, as typically happens when booms are followed by recessions. By October 2010, it had shrunk slightly to 2.3 points, likely reflecting Federal Reserve policies aimed at stimulating economic growth by lowering long-term real rates. However, our analysis suggests that the yield curve in future years will continue to be steeper than in 2007 because of the growing imbalance between saving and desired investment, which increases pressure on long-term real rates.

---

64 For instance, see John B. Taylor, *Getting off track: How government actions and interventions caused, prolonged, and worsened the financial crisis,* Palo Alto, California: Hoover Institution Press, 2009.

65 This is true whether we look at ex-post real yields, or whether we take nominal yields less expected inflation.

One source of inflation concerns today is the challenge central banks will face when the economic recovery gains momentum and it comes time for them to reduce the money supply. Since the start of the 2008 financial crisis, many central banks have injected very large amounts of bank reserves into their economies, both to stabilize their financial systems and stimulate GDP growth. From 2007 to 2010, the European Central Bank, the Federal Reserve, and the Bank of England increased their combined balance sheet assets by $4.4 trillion (Exhibit 33). Once the financial sector recovers and begins to lend more, or once GDP growth picks up, central banks will have to withdraw the excess bank reserves so they do not fuel higher inflation.

Another source of concern is the possibility that China could affect real long-term US interest rates if it decides to rebalance its reserve holdings away from US Treasuries. China's purchases of US Treasuries in the past helped lower US rates.

Exhibit 33

Since 2007, mature country central banks have expanded their balance sheets by a combined $4.4 trillion

Growth in selected central banks' total assets, December 2007–September 2010

$ billion

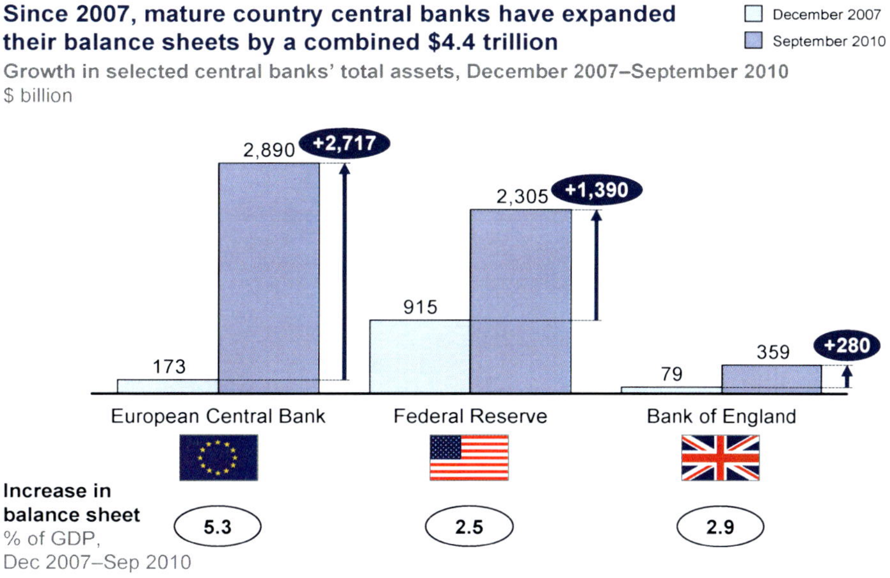

SOURCE: Federal Reserve; European Central Bank; Bank of Canada; Bank of England; McKinsey Global Institute

3.4 GLOBAL IMBALANCES COULD SHIFT, WITH MORE EMERGING MARKETS REQUIRING NET CAPITAL INFLOWS

The coming shifts in the pattern of global saving and investment may also have important implications for cross-border capital flows. As we saw in Chapter 1, differences between saving and investment in any one country give rise to foreign capital flows. Countries with too little saving, or current account deficits, require net capital inflows from the rest of the world to fund investment. Countries with excess saving, or current account surpluses, allow net capital outflows as savers seek investments abroad. In 2009, the United States, Spain, and Italy ran the largest current account deficits. At other end of the spectrum were China, Japan, and Germany, with the largest current account surpluses (see Exhibit 16).

But our analysis suggests that current account balances could evolve in two important ways in the years ahead. First, the largest current imbalances today may be reduced. China's current account surplus has fallen from 11 percent of GDP before the global crisis to 6 percent in 2009. In the consensus global growth scenario, our projections for investment and an assumed saving trajectory in China show that the deficit may decline further by 2030, to 3 percent of GDP or less. Similarly, our projections for investment and saving in Japan and Germany reveal a likely shrinking of their surpluses as well. The US current account deficit shrank from 6 percent of GDP before the crisis to 3 percent in 2009. Sustaining this rebalancing of the largest current account deficits and surpluses once global economic growth rises was one focus of recent G-20 discussions.

A second major change may be in the current account balances of many emerging markets. Contrary to what economic theory would predict, a large number of developing countries have run current account surpluses over the past decade, with domestic saving exceeding investment. This reflects, in part, their response to the devastating financial crises of 1997–98, in which current account deficits and sudden outflows of foreign capital caused severe recessions. But going forward, in the consensus global growth scenario, we see larger increases in emerging market investment rates than in their national saving rates. Our analysis shows potentially larger current account deficits in India and Mexico in the decades ahead, while Brazil's current account surplus may turn into a deficit.

Of course, gross flows of capital around the world will change even more, as they exceed countries' net capital flows by many multiples. But at a minimum, we would expect to see the web of cross-border capital flows grow to include more countries, particularly in emerging markets.

4. Adapting to the new world

Businesses, consumers, financial institutions, investors, and policy makers will all have to adapt and innovate as the world's supply and demand of capital evolve over the next two decades. We could see the end of plentiful capital. Real interest rates might rise. And the locus of saving and investment will shift from the mature economies to the developing world. By 2025, emerging markets will account for more than half of the world's saving and investment. These shifts will require changes in the business models of companies, financial institutions, and asset management firms alike.

We see this report as the start of a global dialogue on the implications of these changes. But it is already clear that governments will need to play an important role in setting the rules that will govern this transition. They will need to coordinate policies, regulations, and actions to minimize potential distortions and sources of instability. The choices made will, to a large extent, determine whether the transition to this new world proceeds smoothly and enables robust growth, or whether it will be laden with pitfalls and missed opportunities.

4.1 BUSINESSES AND FINANCIAL INSTITUTIONS WILL EVOLVE

Companies, financial institutions, and investors will need to update their thinking and strategies to succeed in a world that is moving toward costlier capital and shifting sources of capital supply and demand.

Companies will need a strategic approach to capital

Capital-intensive industries that benefited from falling interest rates and plentiful capital in the past will face higher costs and more competition for funding in the future. Companies that achieve higher capital productivity—output per dollar invested—will have an advantage. They will need less capital for growth and therefore will have greater strategic flexibility. Capital productivity will become an increasingly important top management focus.

Companies with direct and privileged sources of financing will also have a clear competitive advantage. For example, in countries with high saving rates and limits on the outflows of capital, domestic companies may find it easier than their competitors elsewhere to access funding. We can see this today in China, where low-cost funding from the country's banks helps finance business expansion within the country and abroad. However, this lack of competition for capital may result in less productive use of that capital and over-investment in projects with poor returns.

It will be even more critical than in the past for corporations in capital-intensive industries to develop links to large sources of capital. Traditionally, this meant nurturing relationships with major financial institutions in financial hubs such as London, Tokyo, and New York. But going forward, it might also mean building ties with other large pools of capital, such as sovereign wealth funds, pension funds, and other financial institutions from the high-saving countries.

Moreover, for industries whose business models are based on cheap capital, the increase in real long-term interest rates may significantly reduce their profitability, if not undermine their operations. For example, the financing and leasing arms of consumer-durables companies may find it increasingly difficult to achieve the high returns of the recent past as their cost of raising funds increases. Growth will be harder for companies whose sales were dependent on easily available consumer credit. In addition, some types of hedge funds and private equity funds will be challenged. Investment returns in these industries will be driven less by cheap leverage and more by unique insight into industry dynamics and structural trends, and therefore the ability to spot undervalued companies or other assets. For private equity firms, returns also will depend even more on operational management skills that can increase companies' value.[66]

Finally, as the recent crisis demonstrated, companies must realize that short-term capital may not always be available in a capital-constrained world. They should seek more stable sources of funding. This would mean reversing the trend toward the increasing use of short-term debt seen over the past two decades, although doing so would cost more (Exhibit 34).

Exhibit 34

In the recent past, corporate bond maturities have declined, in particular through the rise of commercial paper issuance

Global corporate bond and commercial paper issuance, 1991-2010[1]

Percent of total $ value of bond issuance

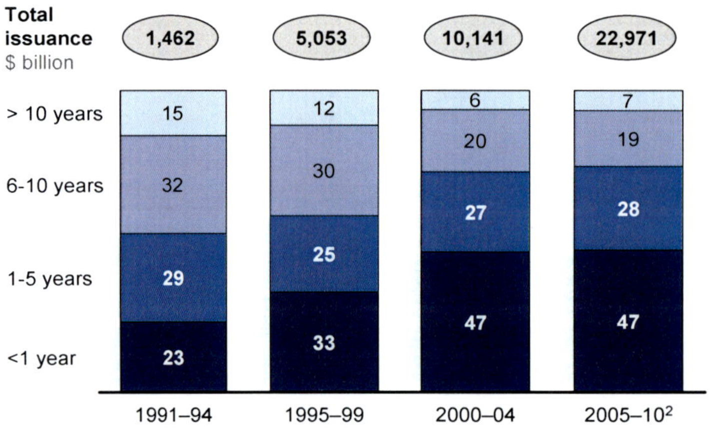

1 Commercial paper data available 1993-2010.

2 Year to date November 2010.

SOURCE: Dealogic; Bank for International Settlements; McKinsey Global Institute

The portion of debt issued for maturities of less than one year rose from 23 percent of all debt issued in the first half of the 1990s to 47 percent in the second half of the 2000s. Financing long-term corporate investments with short-term funding will be riskier in the new world, compared with financing such investments with equity and longer-term funding. To better align incentives, boards should revisit some of their inadvertent biases toward debt, such as using earnings per share as a performance metric.

66 See *The new power brokers: How oil, Asia, hedge funds, and private equity are faring in the financial crisis*, McKinsey Global Institute, July 2009.

Financial institutions will need to rethink their portfolio of activities

Global financial institutions' business models could evolve in at least four key ways as the patterns of saving and investing around the world shift and as interest rates rise.

First, the relative attractiveness of financial institutions' different business lines will change. For example, higher real interest rates may improve the economics of commercial and retail banking. In the new era, credit volumes will likely grow more slowly as higher rates dampen loan demand and as a result of Basel III regulations, but net interest margins may go up because the cost of retail funding typically rises less than lending rates. At the same time, the yield curve is likely to become steeper than it was in the decade before the crisis, as future investment demand pushes up long-term real interest rates. This will make maturity transformation activities more attractive in the medium term. Therefore, after many years in which commercial and retail banking were overshadowed by other bank business lines, this core activity may become more attractive in the years ahead. However, rising rates may also increase default risk, unless banks tighten their lending standards and improve their risk management systems.

Financial institutions' capital market activities may also grow more rapidly than in the past decade. The largest corporations are already increasingly raising funds in debt markets, because they are relatively less costly than bank loans (and this could be even more so under Basel III). An era of higher real interest rates would further fuel this shift to lower-cost intermediation. Moreover, midsized companies will increasingly seek funding through the capital markets, given the relatively higher cost of bank lending due to the new capital regime. This will require innovation within the financial sector to create low-cost options for mid-sized and even small companies to access capital markets directly. Equity underwriting and trading may also increase, if higher-cost debt prompts companies to seek more equity funding, relative to debt, than in the past.

Second, financial institutions will need to build operations where most of the growth in the world's saving and investment is going to occur: in the emerging markets. Global commercial banks, investment banks, and other financial institutions should place greater emphasis on expanding their deposit-gathering and investment activities in developing economies. The largest emerging market countries, with their rapidly growing urban populations, will become increasingly important locations for deposit-gathering and asset management. Cities such as Mumbai, São Paulo, Seoul, or Shanghai may emerge as major new hubs for raising capital and other financial activities. Financial institutions will need to build branch networks or find other methods of accessing savers and investors to tap this wealth. Because emerging market households have lower incomes than those in mature markets, financial institutions will need new technologies, products, and business models to serve them profitably. But competition will be stiff: the leading global financial institutions of today—most of which were historically based in mature economies and reliant on physical branch networks for gathering savings—will be challenged by financial institutions with new business models, as well as by developing countries' domestic banks that already have access to local sources of savings and which have global ambitions. Moreover, foreign banks may encounter regulatory constraints on their abilities to expand their operations in emerging economies, where policy makers saw during the recent crisis how foreign banks can create added risks and higher volatility in capital flows.

Third, banks and other financial institutions will have a big opportunity to develop more instruments for long-term financing and new vehicles for cross-border investing. Investment in infrastructure and real estate is on track to rise both in absolute terms and as a share of global capital investment. These investments are also good hedges against inflation, and thus may be more attractive in the era we are entering. But they require long-term capital and are hard to fund through short-term capital vehicles. Banks and other financial institutions involved in maturity transformation may be ill-equipped to provide the funds needed to meet the increased demand for longer-term investments such as infrastructure, especially given the new capital regime and higher requirements on liquidity. In addition, regulators may constrain banks' ability to raise government-insured deposits in one country and lend them in another. These shifts would exacerbate the challenge of matching global savings and investment in an efficient way. Such moves toward financial protectionism would weaken the prospects for long-term growth. However, these constraints would create opportunities for banks and other financial institutions to create investment vehicles, open to retail or institutional investors, that target particular countries and investments with longer maturity structures and appropriate liquidity terms. Such products will also create new channels for capital to flow from one country to another.

Finally, banks will need to revisit business lines that require high levels of leverage, or in which the end customer relies on high leverage and cheap capital to create value. In a world of costlier capital, such activities could become less attractive, both for banks and for the end customer.

Investors may pursue new strategies

Over the past three decades, falling interest rates led to a significant shift in investment portfolios, away from traditional fixed-income instruments and deposits and toward equities and alternative investments. McKinsey analysis finds that in the 1980s and 1990s, falling interest rates contributed to higher equity market returns because they lowered discount rates and so increased the net present value of future corporate cash flows.[67] During the decade before the financial crisis, low interest rates also boosted the performance of, and demand for, alternative investments such as private equity, hedge funds, and structured products that utilized cheap leverage to boost expected returns.

A higher interest rate environment could reverse these trends, making the risk-return profile of traditional fixed-income investments—such as high-quality government, municipal, and corporate bonds and some mortgage-backed securities—more attractive. In the short term, any increase in interest rates will mean losses for bond holders as the market value of previously issued, lower-yield bonds declines. But over the longer term, higher real rates will enable investors to earn better returns from fixed-income investments than they could in the years of cheap capital. Such an environment also might curb some investor risk-taking in the search for yield.

Rising real interest rates could also reduce the value of equities. This is because a higher real discount rate could result in a reduction in the net present value of future cash flows. For some companies, this fall in valuation could be partially offset by a reduction in the present value of future pensions and other liabilities. An additional effect is that investments could be cut back due to higher hurdle rates, potentially resulting in additional dividend payments or share repurchases.

---

67 See Koller, Dobbs, and Huyett, *Value: The Four Cornerstones of Corporate Finance* (2010).

The world's growing infrastructure investment could be an attractive opportunity for pension funds, insurers, endowments, and other institutional investors with multi-decade liabilities. However, their portfolio managers often make investment decisions under pressure to meet quarterly or annual performance benchmarks measured through mark-to-market accounting. Improved governance and incentive structures will be needed to allow managers to focus on long-term returns instead. This will be especially true for those managing portfolios that have a growing proportion of less liquid, long-term investments, since volatility in prices may reflect market liquidity conditions rather than the investment's intrinsic, long-term value.[68]

Emerging markets may present attractive investment opportunities for financial investors, but there are many risks and complexities, and returns could vary significantly across markets. As emerging markets' incomes rise and capital markets develop, nonfinancial businesses can expect healthy growth from investing in both physical and financial assets. However, returns to financial investors may not be as attractive, particularly in countries where savings are trapped within domestic markets because of capital controls or a "home bias" among domestic savers and investors.[69] These countries will remain susceptible to below-cost-of-capital returns as well as bubbles in equity markets, real estate, and other asset markets, resulting in market valuations that exceed intrinsic value. Foreign investors will need to carefully assess valuations before committing their capital. They will also need to take a long-term perspective, since volatility in these bubble-prone markets may remain higher than in developed markets.

4.2 POLICY MAKERS CAN EASE THE TRANSITION

Government legislators and financial market regulators have an important role to play in facilitating greater global saving and investment. They face policy choices in four critical areas: encouraging more saving and investment in some mature economies; fostering the development of deeper and broader financial markets in emerging markets; creating the conditions that will attract capital to the economies that need it; and enabling international investment in long-term assets.

Encourage more saving and investment in mature economies

Policy makers in some mature countries need to encourage more domestic saving to rebalance their economies and to ensure that there is sufficient household wealth to fund retirement. In the United States, for example, investment has exceeded saving since 1992, with the gap widening over time (Exhibit 35). Greater saving will mean a lower level of consumption, however, and consumer spending has been the primary engine of economic growth for a number of these countries. Policy makers therefore worry that higher household saving—and hence lower consumption—will dampen GDP growth and stifle the recovery. But this is not the case if investment increases—as China has amply demonstrated. Governments in many mature economies should therefore seek ways to address their investment backlog as well as increase saving.

68 See Blackstone co-founder Stephen Schwarzman's comments on mark-to-market accounting during the Seoul G-20 Business Summit, *The New York Times DealBook*, November 11, 2010.

69 The "home bias" refers to the observation that individuals hold too little of their wealth in foreign assets to achieve the full benefits of portfolio diversification. See, for instance, Karen Lewis, "Trying to explain home bias in equities and consumption," *Journal of Economic Literature*, June 1999, volume 37; Harald Hau and Helene Rey, "Home bias at the fund level," *American Economic Review*, May 2008, volume 98; Kiichi Tokuoka, "The Outlook for Financing Japan's Public Debt," International Monetary Fund working paper, January 2010.

Exhibit 35

The United States has consistently maintained a higher investment rate than saving rate, resulting in a large current account deficit

Gross national saving and investment, 1980-2009

% of GDP

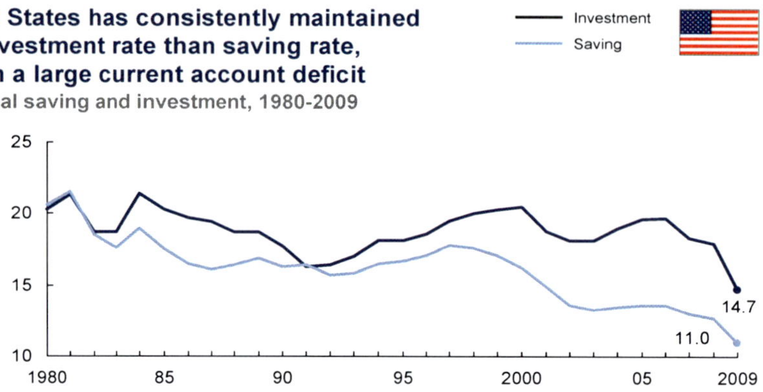

Nominal values, $ billion

	1980	85	90	95	2000	05	2009
Saving	569	731	940	1,224	1,584	1,676	1,569
Investment	561	849	1,017	1,333	2,001	2,466	2,096
Current account balance[1]	2	-124	-79	-114	-417	-748	-378

1 Note that the current account balance does not always equal saving minus investment; see technical appendix.

SOURCE: Haver Analytics; McKinsey Global Economic Growth Database; World Development Indicators of the World Bank; McKinsey Global Institute

Policy makers in countries such as the United Kingdom, the United States, and South Korea should start by putting in place mechanisms to ensure that households save more. In the United Kingdom, for example, the Pensions Commission's 2006 proposals included creating a National Pension Saving Scheme in which employees aged 21 and older without better employer-provided programs would be automatically enrolled, with the right to opt out.[70] These proposals led to the National Employment Savings Trust (NEST) scheme. Starting in 2012, employers will have to automatically enroll all eligible job holders into a pension scheme that meets or exceeds certain legal standards. The total minimum contribution will equal 8 percent of qualifying earnings, with the employee contributing 4 percent, the employer 3 percent, and the government 1 percent.[71] In 2002, the Australian government revised the national retirement fund guidelines, requiring all employers to contribute 9 percent of salary and wages to the fund and placing strict limitations on early withdrawal of these funds by retirees. In part due to these measures, Australia's household saving rate increased from 4.4 percent of GDP in 2003 to 8.0 percent in 2008.[72]

Other policy options for increasing household saving include raising limits on tax-advantaged saving vehicles and tightening consumer lending standards (for example, by limiting loan-to-value ratios on mortgages). In addition, policy makers might reconsider the benefits of mortgage interest deductibility, in those countries where it still exists, at a time of tight government budgets and the need for greater household saving. Policy makers should also try to ensure that households with high debt burdens are protected from rising interest rates. This is especially the case in countries where households have floating-rate mortgages such as Japan, South Korea, Spain, and the United Kingdom. Policy makers could explore ways

70 See *Implementing an integrated package of pension reforms: The final report of the Pensions Commission*, 2006.

71 See *NEST: Key facts and mythbusters*, UK National Employment Savings Trust, 2010.

72 Australia's improved terms of trade also contributed. See Thorne and Cooper (2008).

to encourage homeowners to migrate to fixed-rate mortgages to shield them from higher interest burdens when interest rates rise. This would require the development of more liquid markets in residential mortgage securities, given that it is difficult to fund long-term fixed-rate mortgages on bank balance sheets.

Governments can also contribute to raising gross national saving by cutting their expenditures. Persistently low or negative government saving not only reduces a country's overall saving but also creates expectations of higher future taxes, thus damaging competitiveness.

To replace consumption as a driver of economic growth, policy makers will need to adopt measures to boost investment. There are several mechanisms to achieve this. For instance, governments can increase tax incentives for research and development and other forms of investment. They can foster stronger links between academia and business to support innovation and ensure the private sector commercializes new discoveries, particularly in clean tech, high tech, bioscience, and nanotechnology. Governments also should reach decisions on the future regulation of carbon emissions and mechanisms for carbon pricing, because the current state of uncertainty on these issues is holding back clean-tech investment. Additional growth potential in business services and telecommunications can be unlocked by setting standards, improving workers' education and skills, and providing the required infrastructure.[73] Clearly, governments can also spur more domestic and foreign investment in their economies by making them more attractive to global businesses (whether those businesses are domestic or foreign).[74]

In addition, with interest rates still very low, now is an opportune time for governments to address years of underinvestment in infrastructure. We noted earlier that the United States would need to invest $1.2 trillion more than currently planned over the next five years to renew its crumbling infrastructure.[75] For the United Kingdom, similar estimates indicate a required annual increase of $140 billion through 2015, compared with historic levels.[76] While some legislators may be averse to national infrastructure programs at a time when budget deficits are large, such concerns stem from focusing on the wrong national accounting concepts, which treat economically justifiable government investment as if it were consumption. When judging fiscal discipline, lawmakers, financiers, and international bodies, such as the IMF, should look at government gross saving in addition to the fiscal budget balance. The latter deducts investment and is useful only when focusing purely on debt stability. The former appropriately treats necessary infrastructure spending as investment, which does not lower government gross saving.[77] As part of this change, it will be important for governments (as with corporations) to have some test to determine whether their investments are economically and socially necessary. The G-20 could play a role in helping develop such tests.

---

73 See *Beyond austerity: A path to economic growth and renewal in Europe*, McKinsey Global Institute, October 2010. Also see *How to compete and grow: A sector guide to policy*, McKinsey Global Institute, March 2010.

74 An analysis of how governments can attract corporate investment and enhance national competitiveness is beyond the scope of this research. But see *Growth and competitiveness in the United States: The role of its multinational companies*, McKinsey Global Institute, June 2010.

75 American Society of Civil Engineers, *2009 Report Card for America's Infrastructure*, 2009.

76 HM Treasury of the United Kingdom, *National Infrastructure Plan 2010*.

77 See technical appendix for more detail on the differences between fiscal balances and government gross saving.

Another way to increase infrastructure investment may be through public-private partnerships. Many governments cannot afford to fund all their infrastructure needs with public resources. India is a good example.[78] Some cannot tap global capital markets for financing, or can only do so at very high interest rates. These governments can help meet their country's investment needs by encouraging greater private sector participation. In some cases, governments may have to reform the pricing structures of public utilities or guarantee returns to attract private financing. Policy makers may have to provide stronger legal assurances that private companies and investors will be able to retain the earnings from their investments, and control of their assets. And they must consider which infrastructure investments are going to generate such low financial returns that they must be publicly funded (such as low-usage roads) and which will generate high enough financial returns to attract private financing (such as a high-volume airport).

Create deeper and more efficient financial markets in developing countries

As more of the world's saving and investment occurs in emerging markets, and as global investment demand for infrastructure and other long-term assets increases, the world's financial markets will need new mechanisms to enable the efficient allocation of saving to investment needs.

In emerging markets, governments should promote the continued development of deep and stable financial markets that can effectively gather national savings and channel funds to the most productive investments. Such measures lower the cost of financial intermediation and, by improving the allocation of capital, can promote long-term economic growth.[79] Today the financial systems in most emerging markets have only a limited capacity to allocate saving to capital users. Households still keep a large part of their wealth in real estate, gold, and other nonfinancial assets. We see this in their low level of financial depth—or the value of domestic equities, bonds, and bank accounts as a percentage of GDP and wealth.[80] Governments in these countries should work to develop larger and more liquid corporate bond and equity markets. They must also create a domestic institutional investor base to provide demand for these instruments through pension and insurance reforms. Derivatives and securitized assets are also important because these products are necessary to transfer risks and enable overall deepening of financial markets, although policy makers will want to put in place mechanisms to avoid excessive risk-taking. In many countries, exposing the domestic banking sectors to more competition would improve their operating efficiencies and increase the incentives for them to hone their lending skills.

At the same time, the formal sector financial institutions in many developing countries serve just a small share of the population. McKinsey estimates that 2.5 billion adults don't have bank accounts because they lack access to, or trust in, banks or other financial institutions in their countries.[81] Yet households remain a very important source of saving. This lack of "financial inclusion" means that banks are gathering savings from just a small share of their potential customers. To be sure, new business models will be needed to profitably serve lower-income customers. Policy makers

---

78 See *India's urban awakening: Building inclusive cities, sustaining economic growth*, McKinsey Global Institute, April 2010.

79 See *Accelerating India's growth through financial system reform*, McKinsey Global Institute, June 2006.

80 See *Global capital markets: Entering a new era*, McKinsey Global Institute, September 2009.

81 See A. Chaia, T. Goland, and R. Schiff, "Counting the world's unbanked," *McKinsey Quarterly*, March 2010.

should create incentives to extend formal banking and other financial services to their entire populations. They should also create incentives for citizens to convert their cash and other assets, such as gold, into bank deposits or other financial assets that can be pooled together to fund needed investments in the country.

Finally, policy makers need to ensure that small- to medium-sized enterprises (SMEs) are not disproportionately disadvantaged as capital tightens. The SME sector is the most important source of job creation in most countries but does not have the same access to global funding that is available to larger companies. Indeed, some of the existing regulatory changes, such as Basel III's treatment of trade finance, are disproportionately damaging to SMEs.[82]

Support global capital flows

The analysis in this report suggests that many mature and emerging market economies will need foreign capital to meet their investment needs in the decades to come. Private capital will need to become a greater part of these flows, since Asian central banks' accumulation of reserves have represented a significant proportion of global net flows over the last decade.

Countries that want to attract foreign capital will need to create the right conditions to do so. Foreign investors will be reluctant to put their capital in many emerging markets unless there are instruments for hedging the foreign exchange risks involved. In addition, foreign investors will want assurances that they can repatriate the earnings that flow from their investments, and they will need a legal system that can protect their interests and resolve claims.

Policy makers in all countries should also consider removing limits on the amount that households and pension funds can invest in foreign markets. In many countries, pension funds face restrictions on the proportion of their portfolios that can be invested outside their domestic market. In some emerging markets, households and investors are prohibited from investing in foreign markets. In addition, policy makers should consider removing barriers or regulations that limit or dissuade long-term investment from abroad. Another way to encourage greater cross-border capital flows would be to take steps to reduce investors' "home bias"—the tendency to hold a disproportionate share of financial wealth in domestic rather than foreign assets. Eliminating such rules and biases would enable capital to flow more easily to its most productive use, wherever that may be. It would also reduce the risk that trapped capital causes domestic asset bubbles and keeps currencies out of line with fundamentals.

However, there are risks inherent in a world of more globalized capital markets. During the financial crisis and global recession, we saw how they can increase one economy's exposure to shocks in another. At the time of writing, we are seeing volatile cross-border capital flows drive exchange rate appreciation and asset value increases, potentially out of line with fundamentals. Nevertheless, before the crisis we saw how healthy capital markets help support economic growth and raise living standards by channeling capital from savers in one part of the world to investors who can put it to work elsewhere.[83] Policy makers should therefore strike the right balance between enabling cross-border capital flows and minimizing the instability that comes from short-term volatile movements.

---

82 See *Scaling-up SME access to financial services in the developing world*, released at the G-20 Seoul Summit, by the World Bank Group International Finance Corporation, November 2010; and Stein, Goland, and Schiff, 2010.

83 See, for instance, Henry (2003).

To ensure that cross-border capital flows are beneficial for all nations, a greater level of global coordination by countries will be needed in terms of regulations, monetary and fiscal policies, timing of actions, and communication. National governments largely set the rules governing capital inflows and outflows, but multilateral bodies and institutions, such as the G-20 and the IMF, will also need to play an important role in ensuring countries do not engage in "financial protectionism." Another possible role for these bodies could be to foster agreements to reduce the potential volatility of capital flows, perhaps through tax treatments that vary with maturity.

Enable long-term funding

The global demand for infrastructure and other long-term capital assets will grow dramatically over the next two decades. The recent crisis also showed the dangers of relying on short term sources of funding. To help ensure that such investments are funded with stable sources of capital, governments can take several steps to enable long-term investment.

A variety of government regulations and corporate governance mechanisms provide companies with incentives to use debt rather than equity funding. For instance, interest payments in many countries are tax deductible for corporations, while dividend payments are not. Meanwhile, corporate boards and external analysts and investors focus on performance metrics such as earnings per share, which encourages business leaders to have a capital structure with a greater proportion of debt at the expense of equity. Another example is regulations that favor short-term credit products, such as commercial paper with backstop lines of credit, over longer-term debt.

In addition, regulators need to design rules that will encourage long-term investing and create a regulatory framework for infrastructure funding. For example, European Union policy makers currently are working to craft the new Solvency II guidelines that would generally favor European insurance companies matching their assets with their long-term liabilities. The policy makers should keep in mind, however, that mark-to-market accounting reflects short-term fluctuations in asset values, which potentially overstate long-term risks. Relying solely on strict mark-to-market accounting of assets may lead to overly conservative investment strategies. And that may discourage insurers from investing in infrastructure, large real estate projects, and other long-term assets, even though they would be appropriate given the long maturity of these companies' liabilities. Additionally, capital charge requirements should not be biased in favor of short-term investing, because this would damage the insurance companies' long-term investment model.

□ □ □

As we write this report, global investment already appears to be rebounding from the 2009 recession. The outlook for global saving is less certain. A climate of costlier and tighter credit would challenge the entire global economy and could dampen future growth. However, higher interest rates would be welcomed by savers and could prevent a return to the conditions that fueled the credit bubble. Financial institutions will have to adapt and innovate as more saving and investment occurs in emerging markets. Non-financial companies will have to boost their capital productivity and secure new dedicated sources of funding as capital becomes less plentiful. While leaders must address the current economic malaise, they must also continue laying the groundwork and creating the conditions for robust long-term growth for years to come.

Appendix A: Technical notes

These technical notes provide more detail on some of the definitions and methodologies employed in this report. We address the following points:

1. Capital supply, demand, and real interest rates
2. The relationship between saving, investment and the current account
3. Data sources and classification of countries
4. Investment definitions and data
5. Methodology for estimating capital stock
6. Methodology for projecting investment demand
7. Saving definitions and data
8. Scenarios for future saving and investment demand
9. Real interest rate definitions and methodology

1. CAPITAL SUPPLY, DEMAND, AND REAL INTEREST RATES

Capital markets, like many goods markets, follow the laws of supply and demand. The supply of capital (savings) and demand for capital (desired investment) determine the cost of capital, measured as the long-term real interest rate. The demand for capital depends on the expected returns of investment projects. At the same time, savers' willingness to forgo consumption and supply capital today depends on the returns they expect in the future. If the cost of capital is low, savers require low returns on their funds, and the demand for investment can exceed the supply of (cheap) capital. If the cost of capital is high, few investors can promise such high returns to savers, and demand for (expensive) capital falls short of supply. The equilibrium cost of capital—the real rate of interest—adjusts so saving equals investment.

Shifts in both the willingness to save and desired investment can cause real long-term interest rates to change over time. Demographic changes, income shocks, and government policy shifts can alter savings behavior. Expected returns depend on macroeconomic conditions, labor force dynamics, and technological innovation, which can affect the attractiveness of capital investment. As discussed in this report, during the past 30 years, the large decline in investment demand put downward pressure on the real interest rate.

In a very generalized graph of this relationship, the cost of capital lies at the point where the supply curve intersects the demand curve—where saving equals investment (Exhibit A 1). The falling investment rate in the last decades of the 20th century is depicted by a downward shift in the investment demand curve over time. This results in a lower amount of investment and a lower interest rate, as we indeed observed. As a result of the lower interest rate, saving becomes less attractive and also declines, which fits the observed facts in mature economies.

Exhibit A 1

Over the last three decades, decreasing demand for investment contributed to the fall of real interest rates

Demand for investment and supply of saving

1980 vs. 2008

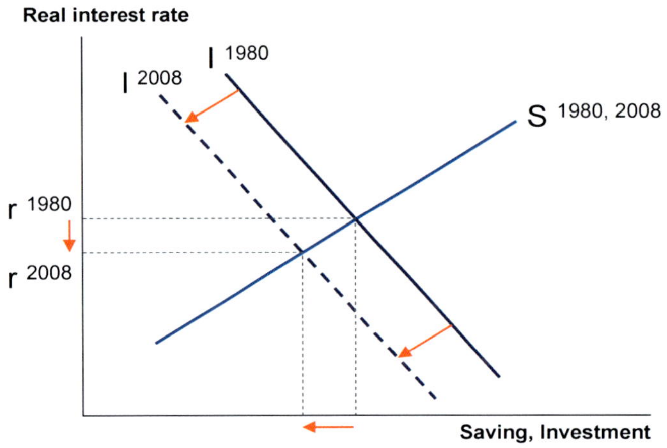

SOURCE: McKinsey Global Institute

Of course, the willingness to save and the desire to invest are not the only determinants of the real long-term interest rate. Investor fears of inflation and country and macroeconomic risk also affect the cost of capital. However, as discussed in the report, the fall in investment demand was the largest driver of the decline in long-term real interest rates over the past 30 years. Moreover, in a world of increasingly integrated capital markets, global trends in saving and investment will determine the real interest rate. Thus, while the supply of savings may not equal the demand for investment in any one country, the real global interest rate will adjust until global savings equals global investment.

2. THE RELATIONSHIP BETWEEN SAVING, INVESTMENT, AND THE CURRENT ACCOUNT

Global saving has to equal global investment. At the national level, however, saving and investment will not always equal one another in an open economy. In this case, saving equals investment plus the current account balance. Whenever a country's gross national saving falls short of its gross investment, it has to borrow the difference from abroad to fund its investment needs. This net borrowing occurs through capital inflows and foreign investment. Because the current account and capital accounts are essentially opposite sides of the balance sheet, the borrower thus runs a current account deficit and capital account surplus. And the current account deficit equals the gap between domestic saving and investment. The opposite is true in countries that run a current account surplus. In these countries, domestic saving exceeds investment, and the result is a net outflow of capital, or a capital account deficit.

In practice, however, current account balances rarely equal the gaps between national saving and national investment because of errors in measurement and different statistical methods in accounting for saving, investment, and capital flows (Exhibit A 2).

Exhibit A 2

In theory, national saving minus investment equals the current account; in practice, accounting methods can create a discrepancy

$ billion, 2008, nominal values

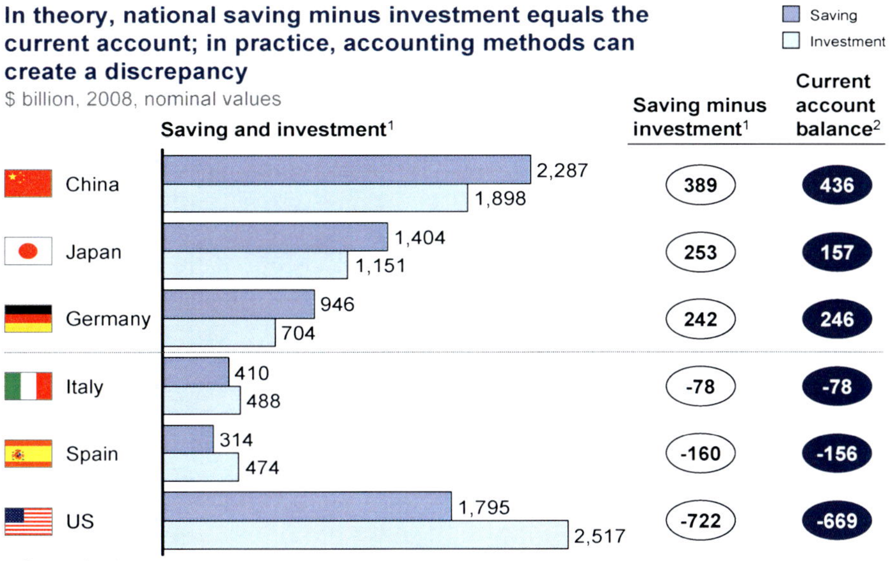

1 From national accounts.
2 From balance of payments.
SOURCE: McKinsey Global Economic Growth Database; McKinsey Global Institute; World Development Indicators of the World Bank

3. DATA SOURCES AND CLASSIFICATION OF COUNTRIES

Our data on GDP, investment, saving, current accounts, and foreign exchange rates come from the McKinsey Global Economic Growth Database. Alternative public sources include the World Development Indicators of the World Bank, the United Nations System of National Accounts, and official national statistics offices, such as the US Bureau of Economic Analysis, the European Union's Eurostat, and Japan's Social Research Institute.

Our dataset comprises 111 countries. We often classify the countries in three groups: developed economies, emerging economies, and oil exporters. We define developed economies as those with an average 2004–08 annual GDP per capita at or above $14,500 (which was the global average), excluding high-income oil exporters. Conversely, emerging economies are those with an average 2004–08 annual GDP per capita lower than $14,500. Our set of oil-exporting countries comprises Algeria, Angola, Azerbaijan, Bahrain, Iran, Kazakhstan, Kuwait, Libya, Norway, Oman, Qatar, Saudi Arabia, Syria, Venezuela, and Yemen.

Additional sources that we extensively used are: Global Insight and EU KLEMS for the split of investment by industry and type of asset; the United Nations System of National Accounts for saving by households, corporations, and government; Global Insight, the Economist Intelligence Unit, and Oxford Economics for the forecast of GDP and the labor force; and the International Monetary Fund's International Financial Statistics and the Organization for Economic Co-operation and Development for interest rates.

4. INVESTMENT DEFINITIONS AND DATA

Throughout this report, we use gross capital formation as the main measure for investment. This includes investment in housing, commercial and industrial real estate, equipment and machinery, roads, railroads, airports, power plants, electric grid, water supply systems, and other infrastructure. It also includes changes in inventories. In line with the commonly used definition of investment in the national accounts, software is also part of gross capital formation. Other intangible investments, such as research and development, education, branding and marketing, patents, and goodwill, are not included. Both public and private investment are included.

Alternative definitions of investment include gross fixed capital formation and net capital formation. Unlike gross capital formation, gross fixed capital formation includes only investment in fixed capital assets, and not the annual change in inventory. Net capital formation subtracts the consumption of fixed capital (the depreciation allowance): thus, it subtracts the share of investment needed to renew depreciated assets. It, therefore, represents the annual addition to the total capital stock. The change in inventory is normally a small share of total investment (3 percent in 2007), while consumption of fixed capital represents 56 percent of investment (Exhibit A 3).

Exhibit A 3

More than half of capital investment merely renews fixed assets consumed during the previous year

Comparison of capital formation metrics

Global $ trillion, 2007, nominal values

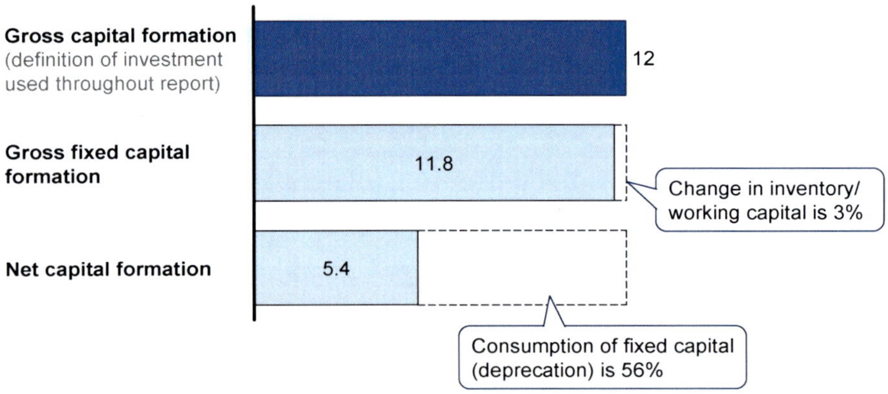

NOTE: Based on data for 101 countries.
SOURCE: McKinsey Global Economic Growth Database; World Development Indicators of the World Bank; McKinsey Global Institute

The share of the consumption of fixed capital in total capital formation is higher for developed economies because they have a larger capital stock and hence more depreciation each year (Exhibit A 4).

Exhibit A 4

In China and India, net capital formation comprises a much larger percentage of total gross capital formation than in developed economies

Comparison of capital formation metrics

2007, % of GDP

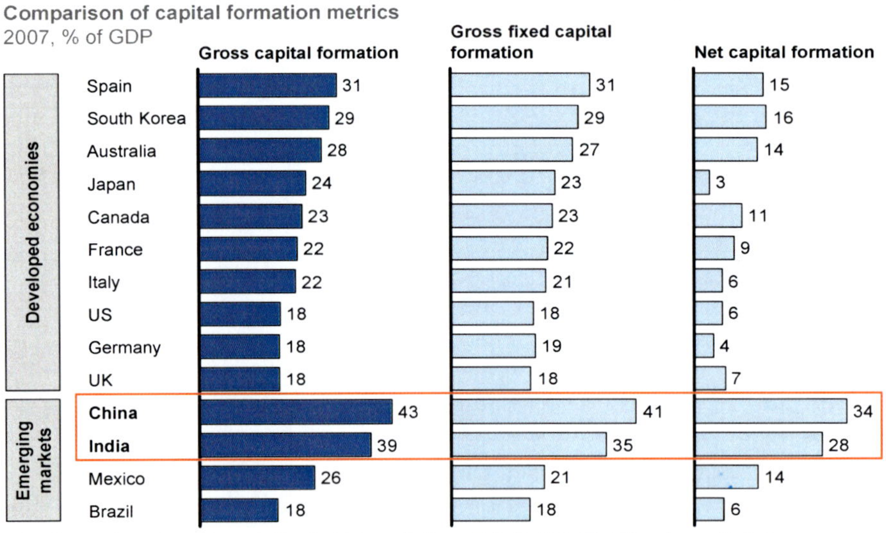

SOURCE: McKinsey Global Economic Growth Database; McKinsey Global Institute; World Development Indicators of the World Bank

We decompose investment for 75 countries into three types: residential real estate, infrastructure, and other productive assets. We estimate the share of each of the three types by adjusting the data series on investment by industry from Global Insight. Global Insight provides historic estimates of investment for 95 industries and 75 countries over the period 1980 to 2008.

A. Residential real estate

To estimate the amount of residential real estate investment in each country, we start with Global Insight's data on the share of investment in the real estate industry. We then estimate the share of residential structures in the real estate industry[84] from the EU KLEMS database for seven large economies (Australia, Germany, Italy, Japan, Spain, the United Kingdom, and the United States). We apply the resulting average share—about 90 percent—to all other countries, since it is stable across countries and over time. Finally, we apply the share of investment in residential real estate to the investment data from the McKinsey Global Economic Growth Database in order to estimate the dollar value of investment in residential real estate (Exhibit A 5).

Exhibit A 5

India, Brazil, and Mexico lag far behind developed economies in residential real estate investment

Investment in residential real estate, 2008
% of GDP

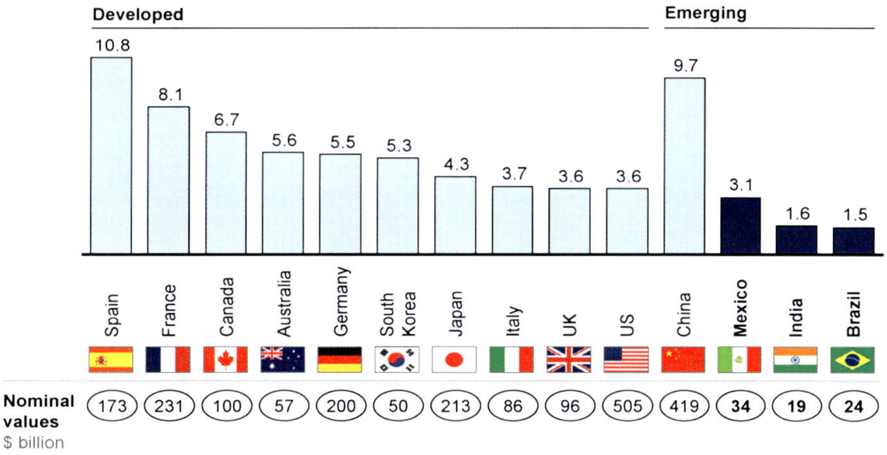

SOURCE: EU KLEMS; McKinsey Global Economic Growth Database; Global Insight; World Development Indicators of the World Bank; McKinsey Global Institute

B. Infrastructure

We define the amount of investment in infrastructure in each country as the share of total gross fixed capital formation in the following industries: utilities (i.e., electricity, gas, and water supply), transportation, and communication. This methodology may lead to a slight overestimate because we include not only infrastructure assets but also all other asset types used by operators in the infrastructure industry, such as commercial/industrial real estate, software, and office equipment. We apply the share of infrastructure investment to the investment data from McKinsey's proprietary database in order to estimate the dollar value of capital spending in infrastructure each year (Exhibit A 6).

84 About 95 to 100 percent of residential structures are accounted for in the real estate industry.

Exhibit A 6

China and India invest significantly more in infrastructure as a percent of GDP than do all developed economies

Investment in infrastructure, 2008

% of GDP

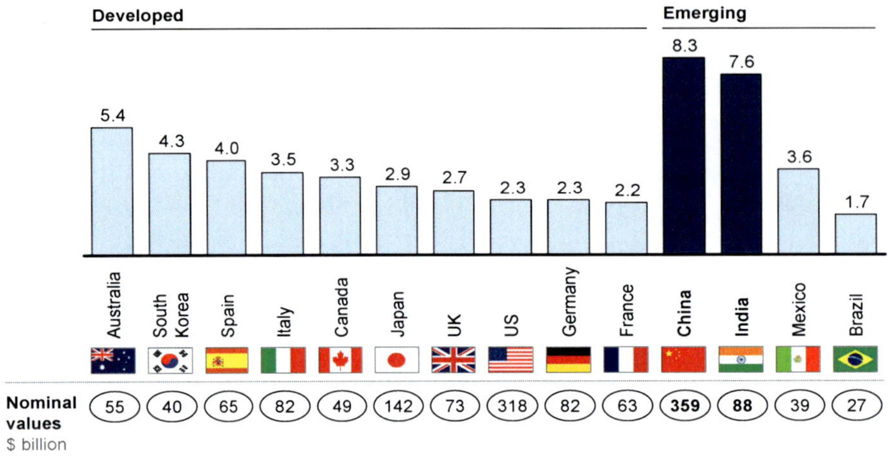

SOURCE: McKinsey Global Economic Growth Database; Global Insight; World Development Indicators of the World Bank; McKinsey Global Institute

C. Other productive assets

The share of other productive assets is total investment minus residential real estate and infrastructure—the investment by all other industries. It includes industrial real estate, office buildings, manufacturing equipment and machinery, mining and oil production equipment, and IT hardware and software.

For specific industry-level analyses, we further break down investment in other productive assets into investment by industry sectors: agriculture & mining, manufacturing, services (including financial intermediaries, wholesale & retail trade, hotels & restaurants, leasing of machinery & equipment, computer programming, research & development, and other business-related services), health & education, and other industries (including construction, public administration & defense, social & personal services, and private household services) (Exhibit A 7).

Exhibit A 7

In 2008, the world invested most heavily in the service and residential real estate industries

Global investment by industry, 2008

%

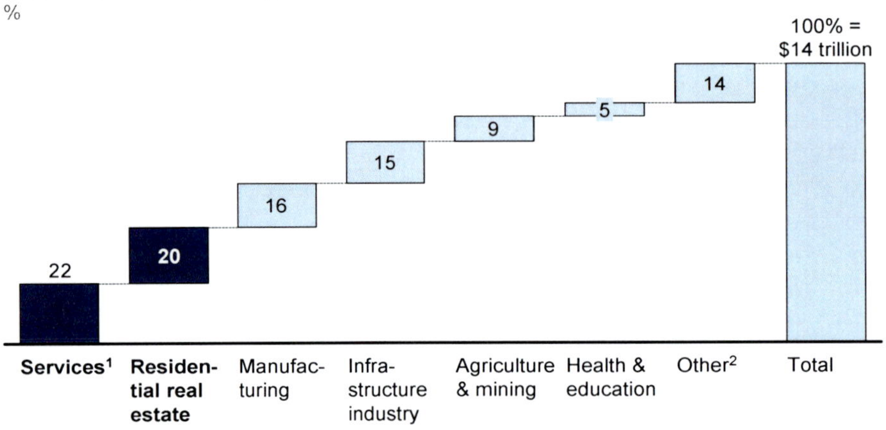

1 Comprises financial intermediation, wholesale & retail trade, hotels & restaurants, real estate companies, leasing companies.

2 Comprises construction, public administration, defense & Social Security, social & personal services, and private household services.

SOURCE: EU KLEMS; Global Insight; McKinsey Global Economic Growth Database; World Development Indicators of the World Bank; McKinsey Global Institute

5. METHODOLOGY FOR ESTIMATING CAPITAL STOCK

We define capital stock as the value of total fixed capital assets at the end of each period, excluding inventories and other working capital. We estimated the capital stock for 75 countries, separating residential real estate from productive assets (both infrastructure and other productive assets). The capital stock is measured using the perpetual inventory method.[85] This method is the most widely used approach to measure a stock of fixed assets. It assumes that the capital stock comes from accumulating the annual flow of investment each year at constant prices and adjusting for retirement and depreciation:

$$K_{i,t} = K_{i,t-1}\,(1-\delta_i) + I_{i,t}$$

where $K_{i,t}$ is the capital stock for an asset type at time t, δ_i is the depreciation rate for that asset type, and $I_{i,t}$ is the real gross fixed capital formation in year t. Thus, the capital stock in any period is the previous capital stock, less depreciation, plus investment at constant prices in that year.

Following standard practices, we construct the initial capital stock for residential real estate and productive assets of each country using a growth rate approach. This method is based on the assumption that investment will replace depreciated assets and add capital to maintain growth:

$$I_{i,1} = K_{i,0}\,(g_i + \delta_i)$$

where $I_{i,1}$ is the real gross fixed capital formation by asset type in year 1, $K_{i,0}$ is the initial capital stock, g_i is the annual growth rate in investment, and δ_i is the depreciation rate. Thus, the initial capital stock is:

$$K_{i,0} = I_{i,1} / (g_i + \delta_i)$$

We assume a growth rate equal to the GDP compound annual growth rate in the first five years of the series based on available data on GDP and investment. For depreciation, we use rates that are common for all countries and constant between 1980 and 2030, although differences may exist in the depreciation across countries and over time. We use a geometric depreciation rate of 2.5 percent for residential real estate[86] and 7.0 percent for productive assets: this leads to a depreciation rate between 5 and 6 percent.[87]

6. METHODOLOGY FOR PROJECTING INVESTMENT DEMAND

In our projection of future investment, we estimate the amount of gross fixed capital formation using a model based on the Cobb-Douglas production function with constant returns to scale. We project investment for productive assets (including infrastructure, plant and equipment, industrial and commercial real estate, IT hardware, etc.) and for residential real estate separately, since real estate assets do not expand the production capacity of an economy.

---

85 OECD, *Measuring Capital Stock—OECD Manual 2009*.

86 Barbara M. Fraumeni, "The measurement of depreciation in the US national income and product accounts," *Survey of Current Business*, July 1997.

87 Caselli and Feyer, May 2007; Terrones and Cardarelli, 2005.

Thus, to project investment in productive assets we use a modification of the Cobb-Douglas function:

$$Y = A\,L^{1-\alpha}\,K_p^{\alpha}$$

where Y is the real GDP net of the imputed residential-housing rental rate (rent-to-value rate), A is the total factor productivity, L is the labor force, K_p is the capital stock of productive assets, and α is the capital's share of output.

Our projection model uses the growth in labor force (i.e., "L" in the production function) and real GDP (i.e., "Y" in the production function) as key inputs. For labor force we build a "consensus" growth rate by averaging annual growth rate estimates from the Economist Intelligence Unit, Global Insight, and Oxford Economics. The growth rates are updated through September 30, 2010. For real GDP growth, we developed three alternative scenarios that we detail in the section "Scenarios for future saving and investment demand."

We then assume the growth rate for total factor productivity (i.e., "A" in the production function) for most countries will be the same rate as in the past. Investment in productive assets is calculated as the change in capital stock (i.e., "K" in the production function) plus the reinvestment to renew depreciated assets. Across all countries and along the historic and projection period, we assume a depreciation rate of 2.5 percent for residential real estate and 7.0 percent for productive assets, an imputed residential-housing rental rate of 5.0 percent of the residential capital stock, and a 33.3 percent share of capital in total output. The model is not significantly sensitive to the assumptions on depreciation rates and imputed residential housing rental rates and only slightly sensitive to the assumption on the capital's share of output (Exhibit A 8). We calculate the marginal productivity of capital by country in 2030: it confirms the common hypothesis of diminishing and converging marginal returns of capital. Finally, we successfully backtested the results of our projections model.

Exhibit A 8

The investment rate forecast is not sensitive to reasonable assumptions about depreciation rates

Global investment[1] demand by year with different depreciation rates, 1981-2030

% of global GDP, constant 2005 prices and exchange rates

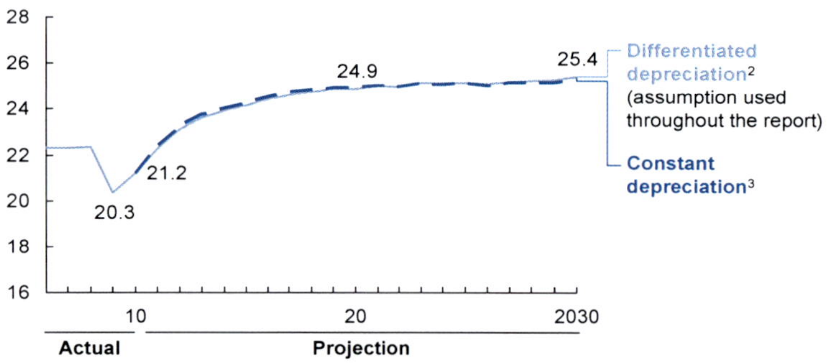

Global investment rate % of global GDP	2010	2030
Differentiated depreciation[2]	21.2	25.3
Constant depreciation[3]	21.2	25.4

1 Data on gross fixed capital formation based on 14 countries (Australia, Brazil, Canada, China, France, Germany, India, Italy, Japan, Mexico, South Korea, Spain, UK, US).
2 Assumes residential real estate depreciation rate of 2.5 percent and productive asset depreciation rate of 7.0 percent.
3 Assumes both residential real estate and productive asset depreciation rate of 5.0 percent.
SOURCE: Economist Intelligence Unit; Global Insight; McKinsey Global Economic Growth Database; Oxford Economics; World Development Indicators of the World Bank; McKinsey Global Institute

Once we have an estimate for productive assets, we break out infrastructure capital spending by assuming an annual growth rate in net infrastructure investment (i.e., investment minus depreciation) and summing the reinvestment to renew depreciated assets (assuming a depreciation rate of 2.5 percent). For most countries, we expect net investment in infrastructure to grow at a rate in line with GDP. For some countries, we adjust the rate slightly upward, anticipating increased demand of renewal of current assets in developed countries (e.g., the United Kingdom and the United States) and of new infrastructure in emerging economies (e.g., Brazil, India, and Mexico). We adjust the rate downward for countries with sustained high infrastructure investment in the past year (e.g., China and Japan).

To project investment in residential real estate, we impute specific growth rates for the ratio of residential assets to total output. These rates are based on the assumption that growth in per capita income normally leads to relatively higher investment in residential real estate. We also take into consideration historic patterns and projected demographic and urbanization trends.

We calculate total projected investment as the sum of the projected investment in residential real estate and total productive assets.

We model investment demand in detail for the 10 developed countries (Australia, Canada, France, Germany, Italy, Japan, South Korea, Spain, the United Kingdom, and the United States) and four emerging economies (Brazil, China, India, and Mexico). These are the 14 countries with the highest real expected GDP by 2020. We also project investment for 65 other countries, aggregated into three groups: 18 developed economies, 35 emerging economies, and 12-oil-exporting countries. For the 18 developed economies, we assume the same growth rates in total factor productivity, net investment in infrastructure, and residential capital-to-output as in the 10 developed economies in our main sample, while for the remaining countries, we use the average growth rate of the 14 countries in our main sample, weighted by GDP.

7. SAVING DEFINITIONS AND DATA

Throughout this report, we use gross saving rates as our definition of saving across the household, corporate, and government sectors. The rates of these three sectors sum to a country's gross national saving rate (commonly called the national saving rate). Gross saving is defined as gross disposable income minus consumption. Gross saving includes depreciation allowances for the expense of the consumption of fixed capital. These are an estimate of the cost of obsolescence and wear and tear of a nation's capital stock and do not lower gross saving. We use the gross saving metric based on national accounts because it must be equal to gross investment in an economy (domestic and foreign), and therefore represents the "supply of capital" available for investment.

A. Household sector

The national accounts calculate household saving as household disposable income less household consumption expenditures. Household disposable income consists of employment income and income from operation of unincorporated enterprises, plus receipts of interest, dividends, and social benefits less payments on income taxes, interest, and Social Security contributions. While earnings on capital (e.g., dividends, interest) are counted as income, capital gains and losses are not. Household consumption comprises spending for consumer goods and services, imputed expenditures such as rent (in the case of owner-occupied homes, imputed rent that they pay themselves as owners of the dwelling), and the production of goods such as agricultural products for final use by the relevant household.

Household saving rates from national accounts can be shown on either a gross or net basis. For this report, we show the household gross saving rate as percentage of GDP because it is a component of gross national saving. A more commonly cited household saving measure is net saving as a percentage of personal disposable income. This is an important measure for understanding household saving behavior because it abstracts from changes in the distribution of national income between labor and capital.

The national account definition of saving is arguably an incomplete representation of the saving behavior of households. For example, the national accounts exclude realized and unrealized capital gains from disposable income. Yet, households typically think of such gains as "savings." Countries also account for pensions differently, which makes cross-country comparisons of both household and government saving more difficult, as discussed below. Finally, it should be noted that the household saving rate based on the national accounts is a "flow" measure and does not reflect variations in the "stock" of wealth of households.

Other alternative measures of the household saving rate are also commonly used. For example, in the United States, the US Federal Reserve's Flow of Funds definition of household saving equals net acquisition of financial assets (cash, bank deposits, stocks, bonds, life insurance, and pensions) plus net investment in tangible assets (residential structures, fixed assets, and consumer durables) less the net increase in liabilities (mortgage debt, loans, and others). Neither realized capital gains (from sale of stocks or a house, etc.) nor unrealized gains (accrued on paper) are included in either definition of wealth. While in individual years the data on household saving in the US National Income Product Accounts and Flow of Funds accounts differ, when averaged over time they are similar.

B. Corporate sector

The national accounts calculate corporate gross saving as the following: gross value added; less compensation of employees, taxes, and subsidies of production and net interest paid; plus net property income received and net other current transfers received; less direct taxes paid and dividends.[88] More simply put, gross corporate saving consists primarily of two main components: undistributed profits (retained earnings) and depreciation. Undistributed profits are earnings that are not paid out to equity owners in the form of dividends. Depreciation is often a large component of corporate gross saving (Exhibit A 9). In the national accounts, depreciation is equal to "consumption of fixed capital" and the rate allowed differs slightly across countries.

It is important to note that repurchase of shares by a corporation are not considered to be a distribution of profits in the national accounts. All else equal, a country with corporations that only repurchase shares would appear to have a higher corporate saving rate than a country whose corporations only paid dividends.

---

88 OECD, *Economic Outlook No. 82*, December 2008.

Exhibit A 9

Depreciation is the largest component of corporate gross saving in most countries

Composition of corporate gross savings of listed companies, 2007
% of total gross savings

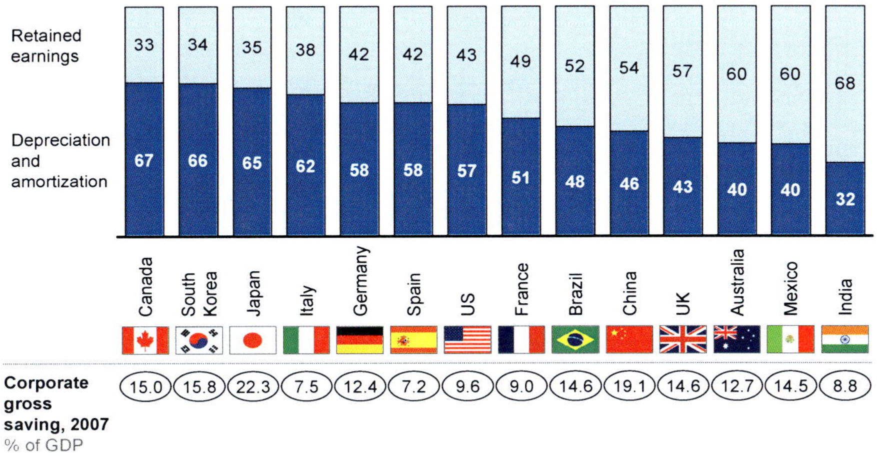

SOURCE: McKinsey Corporate Performance Analysis Tool; United Nations System of National Accounts; National sources; McKinsey Global Institute

C. Government sector

Government gross saving is defined as revenue less expenditures. Revenue consists largely of tax receipts, net interest collected on foreign debt holdings, and contributions to public pensions (if not considered to be a tax). Government expenditures consist of payments for public pension benefits, government operations, debt service, and other public spending. Government spending on investments such as roads and ports are not counted as expenditures (except for the interest paid on debt to finance the infrastructure).

Government gross saving differs from the frequently used metric of fiscal balance. The latter is always smaller because it deducts not only government expenditures from its revenue, but also government investment. The difference between the two numbers is fairly constant. For instance, in the United States it has been between 3 and 4 percent per year since 1980 (Exhibit A 10).

As noted in our discussion of household saving, countries account for pensions differently, which makes cross-country comparison of saving more difficult. The national accounts will ordinarily include public pension contributions and benefits as a part of government revenue and expenditures. All other things being equal, if the citizens in one country rely completely on public pensions and the citizens in another country rely completely on private pensions, their government and household saving rates would be different.

Exhibit A 10

In the United States, the difference between government gross saving and the fiscal balance has remained fairly constant at about 3-4 percent of GDP

Gross government saving and general government fiscal balance, 1980-2010

% of GDP

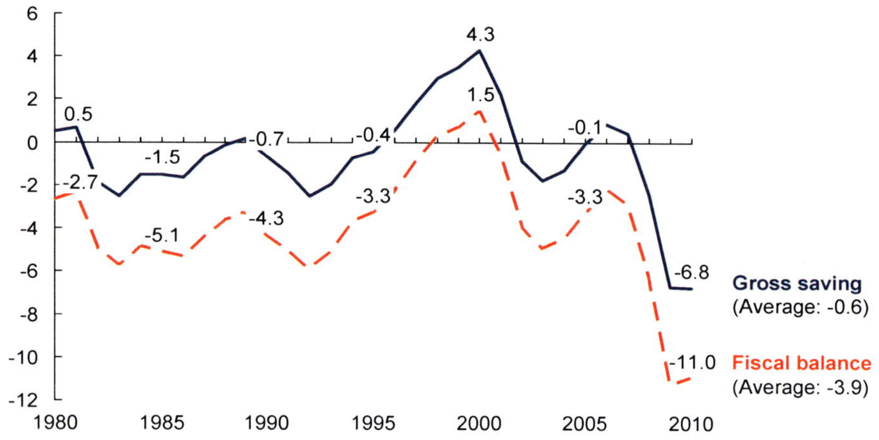

SOURCE: Bureau of Economic Analysis; McKinsey Global Institute

8. SCENARIOS FOR FUTURE SAVING AND INVESTMENT DEMAND

In our assessment of future trends in desired investment and willingness to save, we considered three scenarios of economic growth:

- Consensus global growth
- Weak global recovery
- Slower long-term growth in China and India

Consensus global growth

The "consensus global growth" scenario projects investment and saving assuming a robust global economic recovery from the 2009 recession for all developed and emerging economies. This scenario has a compound annual global GDP growth rate of 3.2 percent from 2008 through 2030. For this scenario, we use the consensus GDP growth forecast created by averaging the estimates for each country from the Economist Intelligence Unit, Global Insight, and Oxford Economics. We use these three sources for making detailed investment projections for the 14 countries in our sample. However, we use only the forecasts from the Economist Intelligence Unit and Global Insight for the other 65 countries because of the more limited geographic coverage of Oxford Economics. The growth rates are updated through September 20, 2010. The consensus GDP forecast has mature economies growing at 2.0 percent annually from 2008 through 2030 and emerging economies expanding at 5.8 percent. In this forecast, the US economy grows at a 2.5 percent annual rate over the period, Japan at 0.7 percent, Germany at 1.2 percent, China at 7.7 percent, and India at 7.5 percent.

China, India, and other emerging economies with high investment rates account for an expanding share of global GDP growth. In this scenario, they drive global investment demand higher over time, from 22.4 percent of GDP in 2008 to 25.1 percent in 2030, at constant 2005 prices and exchange rates.

At the same time, the declining marginal productivity of capital will raise the amount of additional capital needed for each unit of growth in total GDP, leading naturally to a rising investment requirement. Our historic analysis shows that the global marginal productivity of capital dropped at a rate of 0.6 percent per year from 1980 through 2008. In our projections, we expect the marginal productivity of capital to continue falling at a rate of 0.5 percent annually from 2008 through 2030.

In our consensus global growth scenario, we project a saving rate of 22.6 percent in 2030. We calculate this as follows: if we held the 2007 saving rates constant by country, the global saving rate would reach 26.9 percent by 2030,[89] primarily because several big emerging market savers such as China account for a growing share of global GDP. However, several global trends are shaping the willingness to save. In particular, age-related spending is forecast to increase because of demographic trends in many countries. To calculate the impact of age-related spending, we rely on Standard & Poor's projections that national saving will fall by 3.4 percentage points of global GDP over the next two decades. Moreover, Chinese officials have announced plans to reduce that country's current account surplus over time, so we assume it reaches 3 percent of GDP by 2030. The drop in China's current account implies a decrease in its saving rate from 52.5 percent of GDP to about 41 percent, which would reduce the global saving rate by 1.9 percentage points. Finally, we assume UK and US households continue saving at higher rates than before the crisis. We expected the US saving rate to rise from 2.9 percent before the crisis to 6.4 percent by 2010, and the UK rate to increase from 1.4 to 4.5 percent over the same time.

Overall, in this scenario, the global saving rate would be 22.6 percent in 2030. Desired investment would exceed the willingness to save by 2.5 percentage points, or $2.4 trillion.

Weak global recovery

We also consider a case in which the global economic recovery remains very weak for the next five years. Global GDP would increase by just 1.9 percent per year from 2008 through 2015, rather than 2.6 percent, before reverting to trend growth. Although the difference in growth rates may seem small, the effect is substantial because it is compounded over five years.

The "weak recovery" scenario assumes that the US economy grows 1.5 percentage points less per year than in the consensus GDP forecast from 2011 through 2015; China and other mature economies grow 1 percentage point less per year; other emerging economies grow 0.5 percentage points less. Slower economic growth restrains the rise in global investment demand during the five years of slower growth. Although the GDP growth rates would return to the consensus forecast from 2018 on, the investment demand even after 2015 would be lower than in the consensus forecast because the capital stock would be smaller and, therefore, require less annual maintenance. This scenario leads to investment demand of 23.6 percent of global GDP in 2030.

We assume the same saving rates as a percent of GDP at a country level as the consensus global recovery case. However, the global saving rate slightly changes in this scenario because changes in GDP growth rates alter the composition of the GDP weights in 2030. For example, slower growth increases China's share of global

89 We use 2007 because this was the latest year before the financial crisis and recent recession. For oil exporters, we used the average gross national saving rates from 1980 to 2008, because the saving data are highly affected by the volatility of oil prices.

GDP compared with 2030 in the consensus global growth scenario. The US share of global GDP is smaller. As a result, the projected saving rate in 2030 is 22.7 percent, which implies a consequent gap between investment desire and willingness to save of 0.9 percentage points, $800 billion.

Slower long-term growth in China and India

China's economy has been expanding at more than 10 percent annually for most of the past two decades, with growth dipping just slightly during the 2009 global recession. India's growth averaged less than 5 percent per year over the same period, rising to a peak of 7.4 percent in 2008. Going forward, the consensus forecast is that China's annual growth rate will average 7.7 percent and India's 7.5 percent in real terms over the next two decades—still very high by historic standards.

Many possible developments could slow down their economic growth, however. These include urban migration becoming more difficult, an increase in civil unrest, a change in political regimes, or the inability to sustain productivity growth and competitiveness within industries. To model such a "slower Asian growth" scenario, we consider the impact of both China's and India's economies growing 6 percent annually from now through 2030. In this case, investment growth in these countries cools sharply, because slower growth would require relatively less investment. China's investment demand would decrease to about 35 percent in 2030 from 38 percent in the consensus forecast scenario, while India's investment demand would reach about 31 percent instead of 37 percent.

We also project that slower economic growth and lower investment demand in China would affect the saving behavior. We assume that China would not be able to reduce its current account surplus to 3 percent. Thus, for this scenario, we assume the current account will stabilize at 9.5 percent, its level before the 2009 recession.

Moreover, because of slower economic growth, China and India would account for less of global GDP than in the consensus global growth scenario, resulting in lower global saving and investment rates.

Overall, this scenario leads to investment demand of 23.7 percent of global GDP and a saving rate of 21.3 percent by 2030, with a consequent gap of 2.4 percentage points between the world's desired investment and willingness to save, worth $2.2 trillion.

9. REAL INTEREST RATE DEFINITIONS AND METHODOLOGY

Throughout this report, we focus on real long-term interest rates since, in economic theory, the real long-term interest rate is the market clearing price at the intersection of the supply of and demand for capital. Any gap between the willingness to save and the desire to invest will put pressure on interest rates. Over the past 30 years, as the world's willingness to save has exceeded investment demand, there was sustained downward pressure on rates. In the future, we project rising investment demand, insufficient saving to meet the full amount of that demand, and therefore upward pressure on real rates.

We focus on 10-year government bonds issued by the 10 mature economies in our core sample because the weighted average of their yields is an accepted approximation for a relatively risk-free, long-term interest rate. Also, we looked at mortgage loans and medium-grade corporate bonds to better understand lending rates to households and corporations. To compare public and private lending rates and to understand each sector's cost of borrowing over time, we assess the difference, or "spread," between government rates and household and corporate rates. Since 1980, it has been remarkably stable in most mature economies.

Our discussion involves three types of interest rates: ex-ante real, ex-post real, and nominal. Real interest rates reflect the cost of capital, as determined by capital supply and demand, plus a risk premium to compensate investors for the possibility that inflation may rise more than expected. The nominal interest rate is the real rate plus inflation or inflation expectations. It is the stated rate, the one observed in the market.

Real interest rates fall into two categories, ex-ante and ex-post. The ex-ante real interest rate is the anticipated real interest rate in a given year and is a forward-looking indicator. It is very difficult to assess ex-ante rates in the past because calculating them requires an understanding of the historical expected inflation rate and this is generally unknown. We were, however, able to calculate an ex-ante real interest rate in the US using data from the Federal Reserve Bank of Philadelphia. Each year, the bank conducts the Livingston Survey to understand inflation expectations, and publishes the mean result. With this information, we were able to construct an ex-ante real interest rate from 1973 to 2009 by subtracting inflation expectations from nominal rates (Exhibit A 11).

Exhibit A 11

In the United States, ex-ante and ex-post real long-term interest rates show a similar downward trend since the early 1980s

Long-term interest rates in the United States

Yield to redemption on 10-year government bonds, 1973-2009

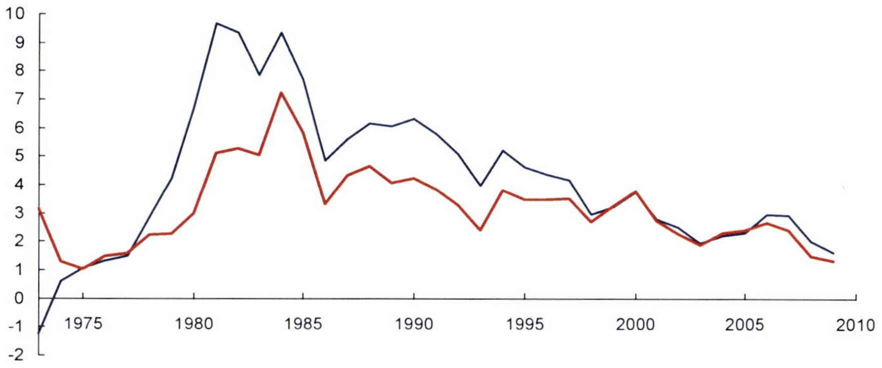

1 Calculated as nominal yield on 10-year bonds in current year minus average realized inflation over next 10 years. We use OECD estimates of inflation in 2009-19 to estimate real interest rates in 2000-09.

2 Nominal interest rate minus 3-year moving average of inflation expectations where inflation expectation is calculated as percent change of mean 1-year CPI forecast from base CPI.

SOURCE: International Monetary Fund International Financial Statistics; Livingston Survey from Federal Reserve Bank of Philadelphia; McKinsey Global Economic Growth Database; McKinsey Global Institute

The ex-post real interest rate is the real rate of return that occured over a specific period of time in the past, accounting for the realized inflation during that period. It is calculated as the nominal interest rate minus the inflation rate for a given period. In this report, since we are looking at long-term ex-post real rates, we subtract a 10-year forward-looking average of realized inflation from the nominal interest rate on long-term bonds and loans. For 1980–2008, we calculate realized inflation as the change in the GDP deflator published by the World Bank. For 2009–19, we use Organisation for Economic Co-operation and Development (OECD) estimates of future inflation.

For our 14-country sample, we looked at the cost of borrowing since 1980. Here we see that both the nominal and ex-post real risk-free rates are at 30-year lows. For the United Kingdom and the United States, we were able to look at a 140-year time series of nominal and ex-post real interest rates going back to 1870 (Exhibit A 12).

Exhibit A 12

UK and US real interest rates varied significantly since 1870; currently, they are at very low levels

Long-term interest rates in the US and UK

Yield to redemption on long-term government bonds,[1] 1870-2009

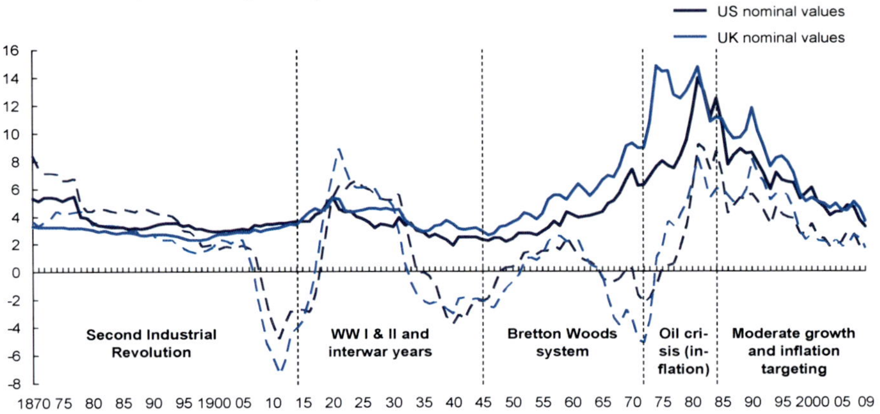

1 US 10-year government bonds; UK 10- and 20-year government bonds.

2 Calculated as: nominal yield on 10-year bonds in current year minus average realized inflation over next 10 years. We use OECD estimates of inflation in 2010-19 to estimate real interest rates in 2001-09.

SOURCE: Ferguson (2008); MeasuringWorth; International Monetary Fund International Financial Statistics; Organisation for Economic Co-operation and Development; McKinsey Global Institute

When trying to understand historical movements in interest rates, we also have examined US Treasury Inflation-Protected Securities (TIPS) and UK Index-linked gilts. These differ from conventional government bonds because they remove inflation risk; the principal is adjusted for inflation every three months. The yields on the inflation-indexed securities show the same decline in real interest rates since 1980 that we see with the yields on conventional government bonds. In addition, the inflation-indexed securities are also useful in understanding the market's inflation expectations: the difference between the nominal yield of a conventional bond and the yield on the inflation-protected bond of comparable maturity and credit quality is the break-even inflation rate. If realized inflation averages more than break-even inflation, the inflation-linked investment will outperform the conventional bond. When realized inflation is less than break-even, the conventional bond will return the higher yield. This break-even inflation figure comprises both expected inflation and the inflation risk premium, but unfortunately it is not possible to separate one from the other (Exhibit A 13).

Exhibit A 13

Inflation expectations in the UK fell consistently until 2000; they have decreased again somewhat since the recession began

Long-term interest rates in the United Kingdom

Yield to redemption on 10-year government bonds, 1992-2010

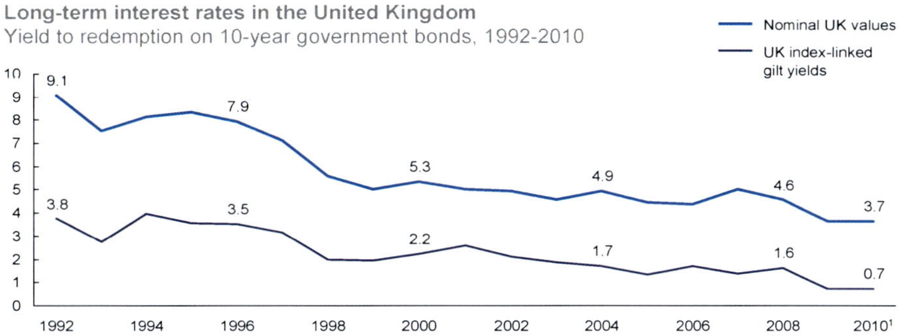

	1992	1996	2000	2004	2008	2010[1]
Break-even inflation rate (expected inflation + inflation risk premium),[2] %	5.3	4.4	2.4	3.1	3.0	2.9
Actual inflation, %	4.3	2.4	0.9	1.3	3.6	2.8

1 Average YTD, September 2010.
2 Break-even inflation calculated as: nominal yield on conventional gilt minus yield of index-linked gilt of comparable maturity. Break-even inflation is a measure of inflation expectations.

SOURCE: Bank of England, Bloomberg, International Monetary Fund International Statistics, Organisation for Economic Co-operation and Development; McKinsey Global Institute

Appendix B: Country detail

In this section, we present historical trends in saving, investment, and the current account balance for each of the 14 countries in our core sample over the past 30 years. While China and India have experienced an investment boom in recent years, investment (as a percentage of GDP) has declined steadily in most mature economies. Saving rates in Japan, South Korea, and the United States have decreased, while saving has exceeded investment in China and Germany in recent years. Greater divergence between saving and investment rates in many countries during the past 10 years has increased the size of current account surpluses and deficits, and thus contributed to global imbalances. Exhibits B 1 through B 14 depict our findings.

Exhibit B 1

Investment continuously exceeded saving in Australia

Gross national saving and investment, 1980-2009

% of GDP

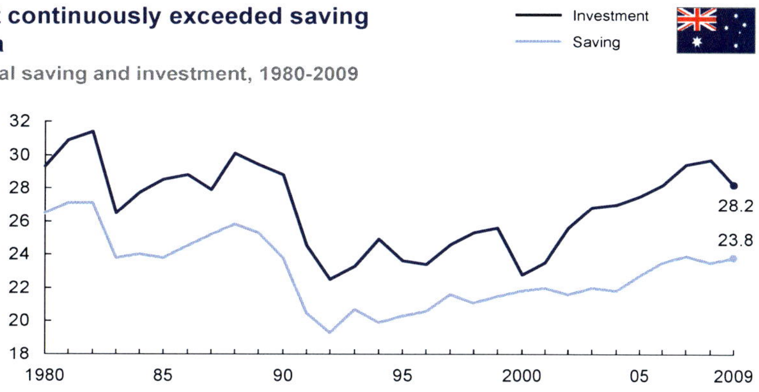

Nominal values, $ billion							
Saving	39	42	73	73	88	153	222
Investment	44	52	91	88	95	192	261
Current account balance[1]	-4	-9	-16	-19	-15	-42	-40

1 Note that the current account balance does not always equal saving minus investment; see technical appendix.

SOURCE: Haver Analytics; McKinsey Global Economic Growth Database; World Development Indicators of the World Bank; McKinsey Global Institute

Exhibit B 2

Brazil's saving and investment rates have been close since 2002

Gross national saving and investment, 1980-2009

% of GDP

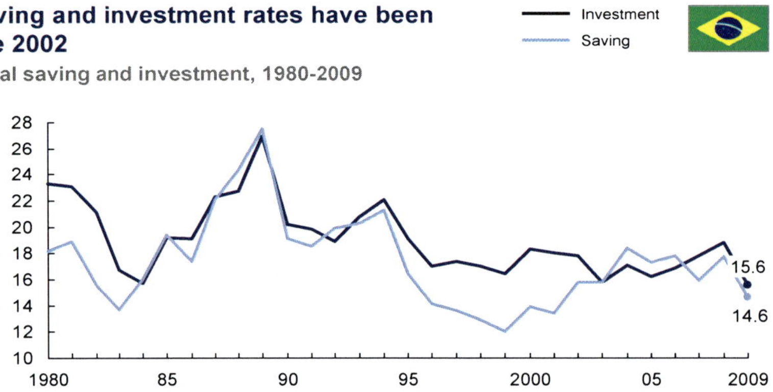

Nominal values, $ billion							
Saving	43	43	88	126	90	152	218
Investment	55	43	93	147	118	143	245
Current account balance[1]	-13	0	-4	-18	-24	14	-24

1 Note that the current account balance does not always equal saving minus investment; see technical appendix.

SOURCE: Haver Analytics; McKinsey Global Economic Growth Database; World Development Indicators of the World Bank; McKinsey Global Institute

Exhibit B 3

Canada's saving exceeded investment from 1999 until the crisis

Gross national saving and investment, 1980-2009

% of GDP

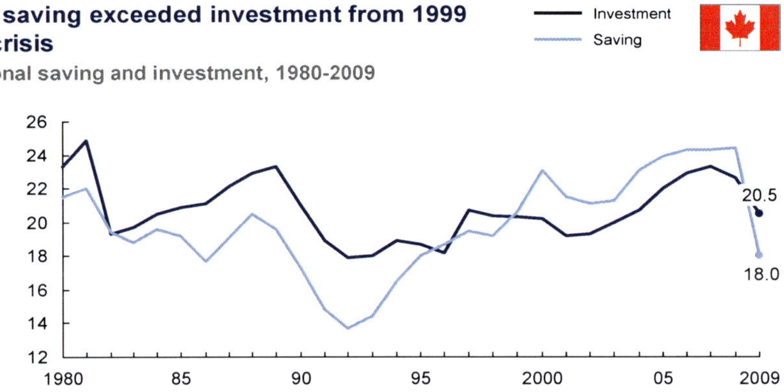

Nominal values, $ billion							
Saving	58	68	101	106	167	271	241
Investment	63	74	122	111	147	249	274
Current account balance[1]	-6	-6	-20	-4	20	33	-23

1 Note that the current account balance does not always equal saving minus investment; see technical appendix.

SOURCE: Haver Analytics; McKinsey Global Economic Growth Database; World Development Indicators of the World Bank; McKinsey Global Institute

Exhibit B 4

Since 1996, China's saving has exceeded investment

Gross national saving and investment, 1980-2009

% of GDP

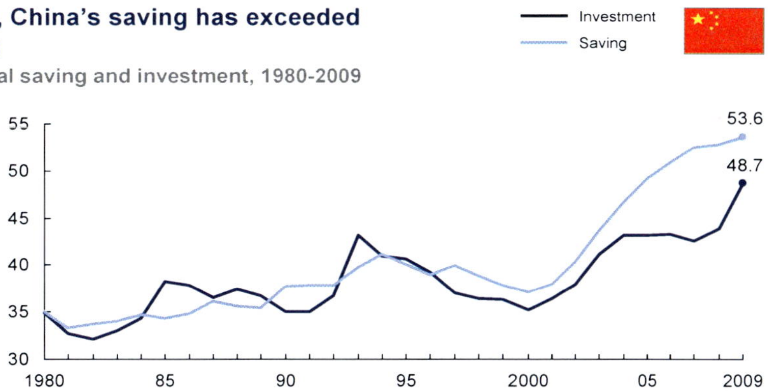

Nominal values, $ billion							
Saving	66	105	135	291	445	1,100	2,518
Investment	66	117	125	296	422	976	2,428
Current account balance[1]	0	-11	12	2	21	161	297

1 Note that the current account balance does not always equal saving minus investment; see technical appendix.

SOURCE: Haver Analytics; McKinsey Global Economic Growth Database; World Development Indicators of the World Bank; McKinsey Global Institute

Exhibit B 5

France's investment rate has exceeded its saving rate since 2004

Gross national saving and investment, 1980-2009

% of GDP

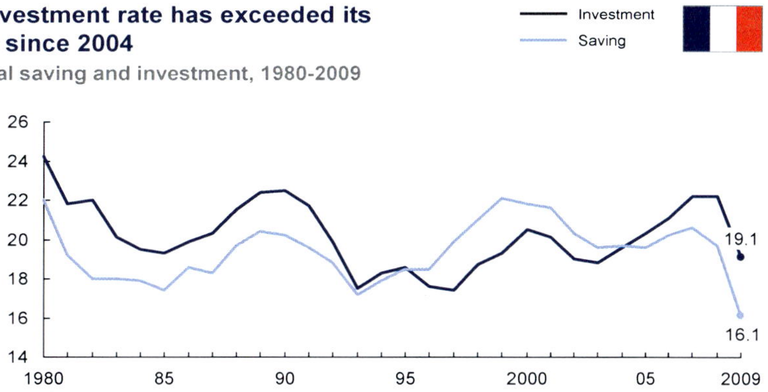

Nominal values, $ billion							
Saving	152	95	251	291	289	420	429
Investment	167	105	280	291	272	436	506
Current account balance[1]	-4	0	-10	11	22	-10	-52

1 Note that the current account balance does not always equal saving minus investment; see technical appendix.

SOURCE: Haver Analytics; McKinsey Global Economic Growth Database; World Development Indicators of the World Bank; McKinsey Global Institute

Exhibit B 6

From 2001 until 2008, there was a growing gap between Germany's saving rate and investment rate

Gross national saving and investment, 1980-2009

% of GDP

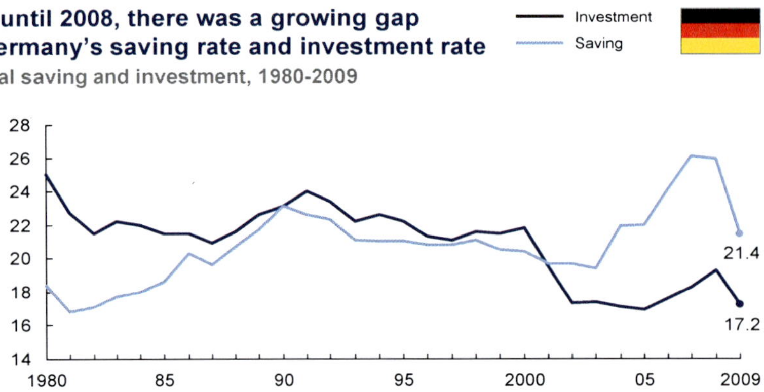

Nominal values, $ billion							
Saving	169	132	395	531	387	615	713
Investment	230	152	397	561	414	471	576
Current account balance[1]	-16	18	-47	-30	-32	143	168

1 Note that the current account balance does not always equal saving minus investment; see technical appendix.

SOURCE: Haver Analytics; McKinsey Global Economic Growth Database; World Development Indicators of the World Bank; McKinsey Global Institute

Exhibit B 7

India's measured national saving and investment rates were very similar until 2007[1]

Gross national saving and investment, 1980-2009

% of GDP

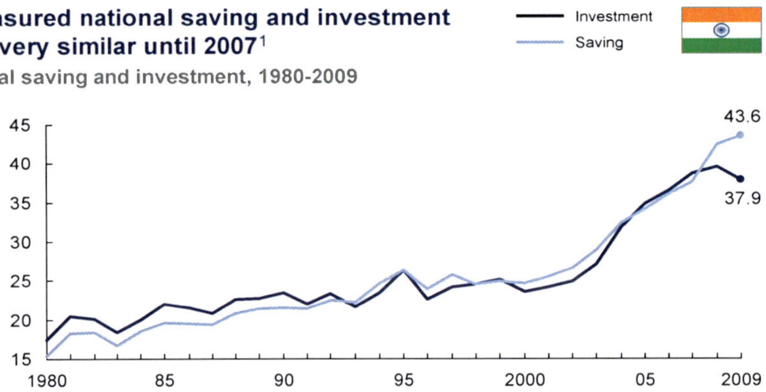

Nominal values, $ billion							
Saving	28	45	68	94	114	276	525
Investment	32	51	75	94	109	292	497
Current account balance[2]	-2	-4	-7	-6	-1	-10	-26

1 For a discussion of measurement problems in India, see Indira Gandhi Institute of Development Research, 2007.

2 Note that the current account balance does not always equal saving minus investment; see technical appendix.

SOURCE: Haver Analytics; McKinsey Global Economic Growth Database; World Development Indicators of the World Bank; McKinsey Global Institute

Exhibit B 8

Since 1999, Italy's investment rate has exceeded its saving rate

Gross national saving and investment, 1980-2009

% of GDP

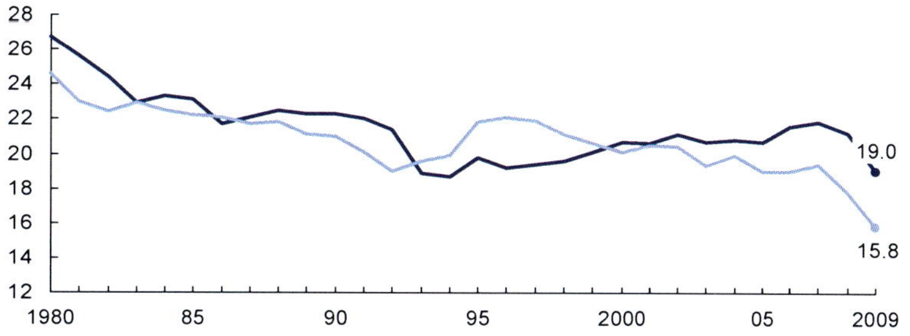

Nominal values, $ billion	1980	85	90	95	2000	05	2009
Saving	113	97	238	246	221	337	336
Investment	123	101	253	223	227	368	401
Current account balance[1]	-11	-4	-16	25	-6	-30	-66

1 Note that the current account balance does not always equal saving minus investment; see technical appendix.

SOURCE: Haver Analytics; McKinsey Global Economic Growth Database; World Development Indicators of the World Bank; McKinsey Global Institute

Exhibit B 9

While Japan has consistently been a net saver, the gap between savings and investment increased from 2002 until the crisis

Gross national saving and investment, 1980-2009

% of GDP

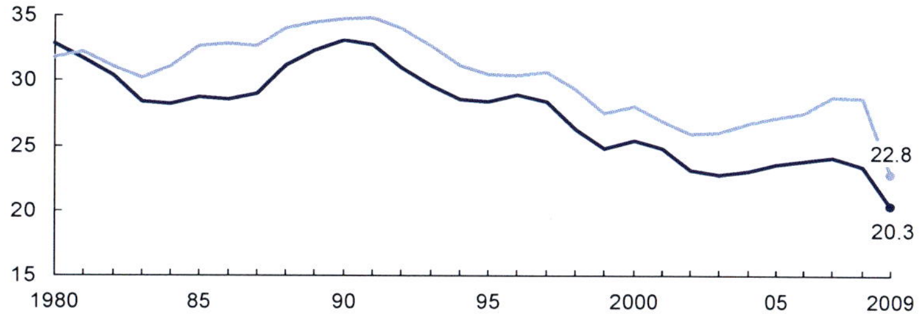

Nominal values, $ billion	1980	85	90	95	2000	05	2009
Saving	336	439	1,046	1,602	1,306	1,232	1,171[1]
Investment	346	387	1,000	1,492	1,187	1,073	1,029
Current account balance[2]	-11	51	44	111	120	166	142

1 Estimated using Japan's current account balances.

2 Note that the current account balance does not always equal saving minus investment; see technical appendix.

SOURCE: Haver Analytics; McKinsey Global Economic Growth Database; World Development Indicators of the World Bank; McKinsey Global Institute

Exhibit B 10

Since the 1997 Asian financial crisis, Korea has maintained higher saving than investment

Gross national saving and investment, 1980-2009

% of GDP

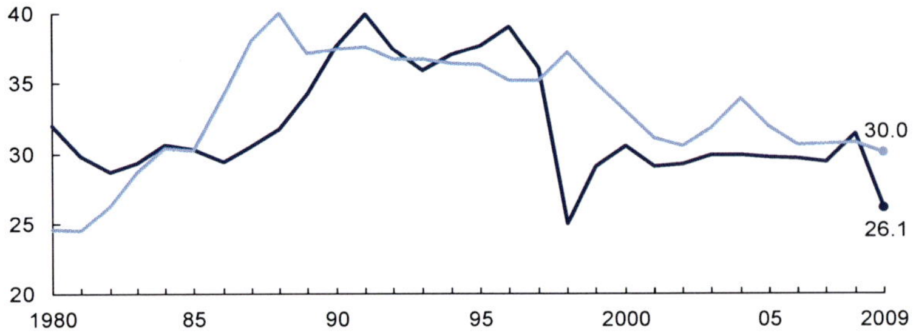

Nominal values, $ billion							
Saving	16	29	99	188	176	269	250
Investment	20	29	100	195	163	251	217
Current account balance[1]	-5	-1	-2	-9	12	15	43

1 Note that the current account balance does not always equal saving minus investment; see technical appendix.

SOURCE: Haver Analytics; McKinsey Global Economic Growth Database; World Development Indicators of the World Bank; McKinsey Global Institute

Exhibit B 11

Mexico's investment rate has mirrored its saving rate since 1995

Gross national saving and investment, 1980-2009

% of GDP

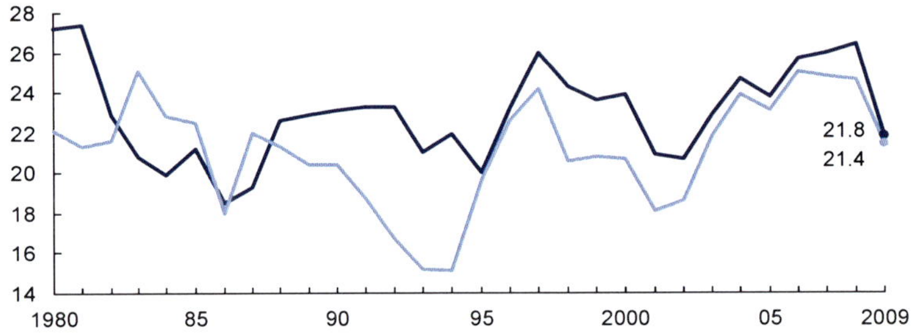

Nominal values, $ billion							
Saving	43	42	54	56	120	196	182
Investment	53	39	61	57	139	202	191
Current account balance[1]	-10	1	-7	-2	-19	-5	-5

1 Note that the current account balance does not always equal saving minus investment; see technical appendix.

SOURCE: Haver Analytics; McKinsey Global Economic Growth Database; World Development Indicators of the World Bank; McKinsey Global Institute

Exhibit B 12

In recent years Spain's investment rate has exceeded its saving rate by nearly 10 percentage points, creating a large current account deficit

Gross national saving and investment, 1980-2009

% of GDP

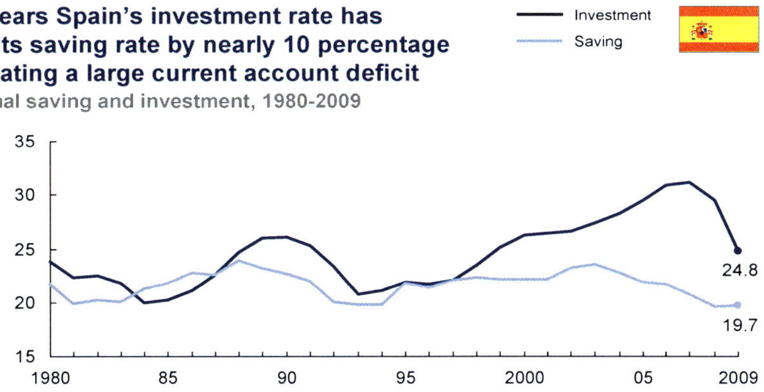

Nominal values, $ billion							
Saving	49	38	119	130	129	248	287
Investment	54	36	136	131	153	333	362
Current account balance[1]	-6	3	-18	-2	-23	-83	-80

1 Note that the current account balance does not always equal saving minus investment; see technical appendix.

SOURCE: Haver Analytics; McKinsey Global Economic Growth Database; World Development Indicators of the World Bank; McKinsey Global Institute

Exhibit B 13

The United Kingdom's investment rate has exceeded its saving rate since 1998

Gross national saving and investment, 1980-2009

% of GDP

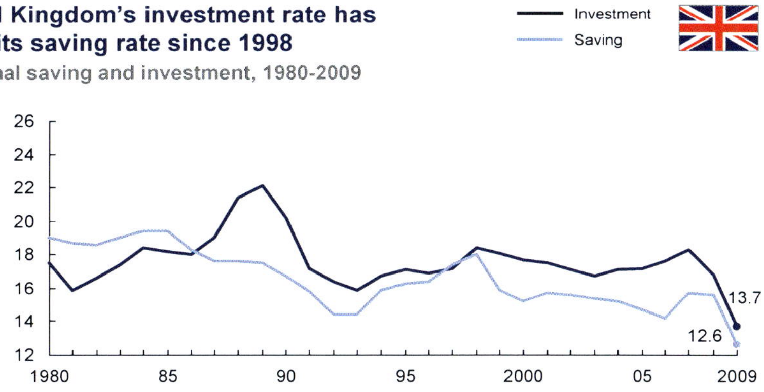

Nominal values, $ billion							
Saving	103	90	169	189	224	336	274
Investment	95	85	204	198	261	393	298
Current account balance[1]	7	3	-39	-14	-37	-59	-24

1 Note that the current account balance does not always equal saving minus investment; see technical appendix.

SOURCE: Haver Analytics; McKinsey Global Economic Growth Database; World Development Indicators of the World Bank; McKinsey Global Institute

Exhibit B 14

The United States has consistently maintained a higher investment rate than saving rate, resulting in a large current account deficit

Gross national saving and investment, 1980-2009

% of GDP

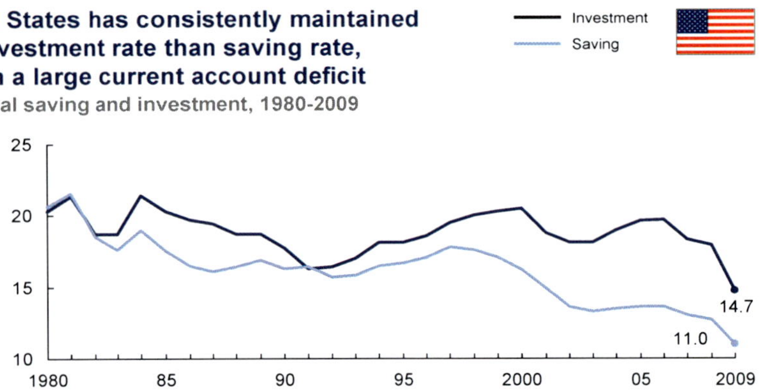

Nominal values, $ billion							
Saving	569	731	940	1,224	1,584	1,676	1,569
Investment	561	849	1,017	1,333	2,001	2,466	2,096
Current account balance[1]	2	-124	-79	-114	-417	-748	-378

1 Note that the current account balance does not always equal saving minus investment; see technical appendix.

SOURCE: Haver Analytics; McKinsey Global Economic Growth Database; World Development Indicators of the World Bank; McKinsey Global Institute

Bibliography

Aaberage, Rolf, and Yu Zhu, "The pattern of household savings during a hyperinflation: The case of urban China in the late 1980s," *Review of Income and Wealth*, Series 47, Number 2, June 2001.

Abdih, Yasser, and Evan Tanner, "Frugality: Are we fretting too much? Household saving and assets in the United States," International Monetary Fund (IMF) working paper 197, September 2009.

Agrawal, Raj, Stephen Findley, Sean Greene, Kathryn Huang, Aly Jeddy, William W. Lewis, and Markus Petry, "Capital productivity: Why the US leads and why it matters," *McKinsey Quarterly*, August 1996.

Agrawal, Shardul, and Samuel Fankhauser, eds., *Economic aspects of adaptation to climate change: Costs, benefits, and policy instruments*, Organisation for Economic Co-operation and Development (OECD), Paris, 2008.

Allais, Olivier, Loïc Cadiou, and Stéphane Dées, *Defining consumption behavior in a multi-country model*, Centre d'Etudes Prospectives et d'Informations Internationales (CEPII), 2001–2002.

American Society of Civil Engineers, *2009 Report Card for America's Infrastructure*, 2009.

Atkins, Charles, and Susan Lund, "The economic impact of increased US savings," *McKinsey on Finance*, Number 31, Spring 2009.

Auerbach, Alan J., and Kevin Hassett, "Corporate savings and shareholder consumption," National Bureau of Economic Research (NBER) working paper series 2994, June 1991.

Authers, John, *The Fearful Rise of Markets: Global Bubbles, Synchronized Meltdowns, and How to Prevent Them in the Future*, Upper Saddle River, New Jersey: FT Press, 2010.

Bai, Chong-En, Chang-Tai Hsieh, and Yingyi Qian, "The return to capital in China," *Brookings Papers on Economic Activity*, Number 2, 2006.

Balassa, Bela, "The purchasing-power parity doctrine: A reappraisal," *Journal of Political Economy*, Volume 72, 1964.

Baldacci, Emanuele, Giovanni Callegari, David Coady, Ding Ding, Manmohan Kumar, Pietro Tommasino, and Jaejoon Woo, "Public expenditures on social programs and household consumption in China," IMF working paper 69, March 2010.

Barclays, *Equity Gilt Study*, February 2010.

Barnett, Steven, and Ray Brooks, "China: Does government health and education spending boost consumption?" IMF working paper 16, January 2010.

Bartzsch, Nikolaus, *Precautionary saving and income uncertainty in Germany—new evidence from microdata*, Deutsche Bundesbank discussion paper series 1, Number 44, 2006.

Bates, Thomas W., Kathleen M. Kahle, and René M. Stulz, "Why do US firms hold so much more cash than they used to?," *The Journal of Finance*, Volume 64, Number 5, October 2009.

Beaton, Kimberly, "Credit constraints and consumer spending," Bank of Canada, working paper 2009–25, September 2009.

Bernanke, Ben S., *The Global Saving Glut and the US Current Account Deficit*, remarks at the Sandridge Lecture, Virginia Association of Economics, Richmond, The Federal Reserve Board, March 10, 2005.

Bonham, Carl, and Calla Wiemer, "Chinese saving dynamics: The impact of GDP growth and the dependent share," Economic Research Organization at the University of Hawaii (UHERO), working paper 19, July 29, 2010.

Börsch-Supan, Axel, *From Public Pension to Private Savings: The Current Pension Reform Process in Europe*, presented at conference on the Economics of an Ageing Society: "The Future of Funded Systems," Rüschlikon, Switzerland, November 2003.

Börsch-Supan, Axel, ed., *Life-Cycle Savings and Public Policy: A Cross-National Study of Six Countries*, Elsevier, 2003.

Bosworth, Barry P., Ralph C. Bryant, and Gary Burtless, *The impact of aging on financial markets and the economy: A survey*, The Brookings Institution, July 2004.

Bosworth, Barry P., *Why don't Americans save?*, The Brookings Institution, August 10, 2004.

Bosworth, Barry P., and Lisa Bell, *The decline in household saving: What can we learn from survey data?*, The Brookings Institution, August 2005.

Bosworth, Barry P., and Gabriel Chodorow-Reich, *Saving and demographic change: The global dimension*, The Brookings Institution, November 2006.

Bosworth, Barry P., and Rosanna Smart, "The wealth of older Americans and the sub-prime debacle," Center for Retirement Research at Boston College, working paper 21, November 2009.

Brady, Peter J., *Optimal savings: Would we know it if we saw it?*, March 2007.

Brooks, Robin, *Population aging and global capital flows in a parallel universe*, IMF staff papers, Volume 50, Number 2, 2003.

Bryant, Ralph C., *Cross-Border Macroeconomic Implications of Demographic Change*, presented at the Federal Reserve Bank of Kansas City's symposium, Global Demographic Change: Economic Impacts and Policy Challenges, Jackson Hole, Wyoming, August 2004.

Bryant, Ralph C., "Demographic influences on saving-investment balances in developing and developed economies," Boston Center for Retirement Research working paper 8, April 2007.

Bu, Yisheng, *Fixed Capital Stock Depreciation in Developing Countries: Some Evidence from Firm Level Data*, Liberty Mutual Group, 2004.

Caballero, Ricardo J., Emmanuel Farhi, and Pierre-Olivier Gourinchas, "An equilibrium model of 'global imbalances' and low interest rates," *American Economic Review*, Volume 98, Number 1, March 2008.

Caballero, Ricardo J., "The 'other' imbalance and financial crisis," NBER working paper 15636, January 2010.

Campbell, David W., and Wako Watanbe, "Will the future Japanese and US personal saving rates be relatively equivalent?," Center for Japan-US Business and Economic Studies working paper 9, September 2009.

Cardarelli, Roberto, and Kenichi Ueda, "Awash with cash: Why are corporate savings so high?," chapter IV, *IMF World Economic Outlook*, April 2006.

Carroll, Christopher D., Misuzu Otsuka, and Jirka Slacalek, *How large is the housing wealth effect? A new approach*, prepared for an Academic Consultants' meeting of the Board of Governors of the Federal Reserve System, January 2004.

Caselli, Franco, and James Feyer, "The marginal product of capital," *The Quarterly Journal of Economics*, May 2007.

Cecchetti, Stephen G., M. S. Mohanty, and Fabrizio Zampolli, "The future of public debt: Prospects and implications," BIS working paper 300, March 2010.

Chamon, Marcos, and Eswar Prasad, "Why are saving rates of urban households in China rising?," NBER working paper 14546, December 2008.

Chou, Shin-Yi, Jin-Tan Liu, and James K. Hammitt, "National health insurance and precautionary saving: Evidence from Taiwan," *Journal of Public Economics*, Volume 87, 2003.

Chung, Kyuil, "Household debt, the savings rate and monetary policy: The Korean experience," Bank for International Settlements (BIS) working paper 46, May 2009.

Clements, Benedict, Victoria Perry, and Juan Toro, *From Stimulus to Consolidation: Revenue and Expenditure Policies in Advanced and Emerging Economies*, IMF Fiscal Affairs Department, April 2010.

Congressional Budget Office (CBO), *The Long-Term Budget Outlook*, June 2010.

Cooper, Richard N., "Living with global imbalances," *Brookings Papers on Economic Activity*, Number 2, 2007.

Cooper, Richard N., "Global imbalances: Globalization, demography, and sustainability," *Journal of Economic Perspectives*, Volume 22, Number 3, Summer 2008.

Corneo, Giacomo, Matthias Keese, and Carsten Schröder, "The effect of saving subsidies on household saving: Evidence from Germany," discussion paper 3, Free University Berlin, School of Business & Economics, 2010.

Corporate savings and rebalancing in Asia, presentation for OECD-ADBI 11th Roundtable on Capital Market Reform in Asia, February 22–23, 2010, Tokyo, Japan, adapted from Sonali Jain-Chandra, Malhar Nabar, and Nathan Porter, "Corporate savings and rebalancing in Asia," IMF Asia and Pacific Department, *Regional Economic Outlook*, October 2009.

Corrado, Carol A., Charles R. Hulten, and Daniel E. Sichel, "Intangible capital and US economic growth," *Review of Income and Wealth*, Volume 55, Number 3, September 2009.

Cottarelli, Carlo, and Andrea Schaechter, "Long-term trends in public finances in the G-7 economies," IMF Fiscal Affairs Department staff position note, September 2010.

Cristadoro, Riccardo, and Daniela Marconi, "Rural and urban households savings in China under different policy scenarios," *Journal of Chinese Economic and Business Studies*, 2010.

Crook, Jonathan, and Stefan Hochguertel, "US and European household debt and credit constraints," Tinbergen Institute discussion paper 87, 2007.

Daly, Kevin, and Ben Broadbent, "The savings glut, the return on capital and the rise in risk aversion," Goldman Sachs Global Economics, Commodities and Strategy Research working paper 185, May 2009.

Davies, Christopher, Valerie Fender, and Barry Williams, "Recent developments in the household saving ratio," *Economic & Labour Market Review*, Volume 4, Number 5, May 2010.

De Serres, Alain, and Florian Pelgrin, "The decline in private saving rates in the 1990s in OECD countries: How much can be explained by non-wealth determinants?," *OECD Economic Studies*, Volume 1, Number 36, 2003.

Desroches, Brigitte, and Michael Francis, "Global savings, investment, and world real interest rates," *Bank of Canada Review*, Winter 2006–2007.

Dewen, Wang, "Can social security boost domestic consumption in the People's Republic of China?," Asian Development Bank Institute (ADBI) working paper 215, May 2010.

Dobrescu, Loretti I., Laurence J. Kotlikoff, and Alberto F. Motta, "Why aren't developed countries saving?," NBER working paper 14580, December 2008.

Economic Report of the President, The White House, Council of Economic Advisers, Washington DC, February 2010.

El-Erian, Mohamed A., *When Markets Collide: Investment Strategies for the Age of Global Economic Change*, New York: McGraw-Hill, 2008.

Enkvist, Per-Anders, Jens Dinkel, and Charles Lin, *Impact of the financial crisis on carbon economics: Version 2.1 of the global greenhouse gas abatement cost curve*, McKinsey & Company, August 24, 2010.

Farrell, Diana, and Ezra Greenberg, "The economic impact of an aging Japan," *McKinsey Quarterly*, May 2005.

Farrell, Diana, Susan Lund, and Leo Puri, "India's financial system: More market, less government," *McKinsey Quarterly*, August 2006.

Federal Reserve Bank of San Francisco (FRBSF), *US household deleveraging and future consumption growth*, economic letter number 16, May 15, 2009.

Fehr, Hans, Sabine Jokisch, and Laurence J. Kotlikoff, "Will China eat our lunch or take us to dinner? Simulating the transition paths of the US, EU, Japan, and China," NBER working paper 11668, September 2005.

Feldstein, Martin S., "The return of saving," *Foreign Affairs*, Volume 85, Number 3, May/June 2006.

Feldstein, Martin S., "Resolving the global imbalance: The dollar and the US saving rate," NBER working paper 13952, 2008.

Felipe, Jesus, Kristine Kintanar, and Joseph Anthony Lim, "Asia's current account surplus: Savings glut or investment drought?," *Asian Development Review*, Volume 23, Number 1, 2006.

Ferguson, Niall, *The Ascent of Money: A Financial History of the World*, New York: Penguin Press, 2008.

Ferrucci, Gianluigi, and Cesar Miralles, "Saving behavior and global imbalances: The role of emerging market economies," European Central Bank, Eurosystem working paper series 842, December 2007.

Financial Services Authority (FSA), *The Turner Review: A regulatory response to the global banking crisis*, March 2009.

Fraumeni, Barbara M., "The measurement of depreciation in the US national income and product accounts," *Survey of Current Business*, July 1997.

Goedhart, Marc H., Timothy M. Koller, and Zane D. Williams, "The real cost of equity," *McKinsey on Finance*, Autumn 2002.

Gramlich, Edward M., "Infrastructure investment: A review essay," *Journal of Economic Literature*, Volume 32, Number 3, September 1994.

Gutierrez, Carlos M., Cynthia A. Glassman, J. Steven Landefeld, and Rosemary D. Marcuss, *Measuring the economy: A primer on GDP and the national income and product accounts*, US Bureau of Economic Analysis (BEA), September 2007.

Ha, Joonkyung, Jong-Wha Lee, and Lea Sumulong, "Rebalancing growth in the Republic of Korea," Asian Development Bank Institute (ADBI) working paper 224, July 2010.

He, Xinhua, and Yongfu Cao, "Understanding high saving rate in China," *China & World Economy*, Volume 15, Number 1, 2007.

Heim, John J., "The consumption function," Rensselaer working papers in Economics 805, January 2008.

Helliwell, John F., "Demographic changes and international factor mobility," NBER working paper 10945, December 2004.

Henry, Peter Blair, "Capital account liberalization, the cost of capital, and economic growth," *American Economic Review*, Volume 93, Number 2, May 2003.

HM Treasury of the United Kingdom, *National Infrastructure Plan 2010*, October 2010.

Hoenig, Thomas M., "The high cost of exceptionally low rates," *Bank for International Settlements Review*, Number 88, June 2010.

Horioka, Charles Yuji, and Junmin Wan, "The determinants of household saving in China: A dynamic panel analysis of provinicial data," NBER working paper 12723, December 2006.

Horioka, Charles Yuji, Wataru Suzuki, and Tatsuo Hatta, "Aging, savings, and public pensions in Japan," *Asian Economic Policy Review*, Volume 2, Number 2, 2007.

Horioka, Charles Yuji, *Household saving in Japan and China*, Institute of Social and Economic Research Osaka University, presented at Doshisha University, June 15, 2007.

Hüfner, Felix, and Isabell Koske, "Explaining household saving rates in G7 countries: Implications for Germany," OECD Economics Department working paper 754, March 2010.

Hung, Juann, and Rong Qian, *Why is China's saving rate so high? A comparative study of cross-country panel data*, presented at conference, "The Evolving Role of China in the Global Economy," Center for Economic Studies (CES) Venice Summer Institute, July 23–34, 2010.

Hurd, Michael, and Susann Rohwedder, "The retirement consumption puzzle: Actual spending change in panel data," RAND Labor and Population working paper 563, April 2008.

Kuijs, Louis, "How will China's saving-investment balance evolve?," World Bank Policy Research working paper 3958, July 2006.

IMF, *Regional economic outlook: Asia and Pacific*, IMF World Economic and Financial Surveys, May 2009.

IMF, *World economic outlook*, IMF World Economic and Financial Surveys, April 2010.

IMF, *Fiscal monitor: Navigating the fiscal challenges ahead*, IMF Fiscal Affairs Department, May 2010.

IMF, *Global financial stability report: Sovereigns, funding, and systematic liquidity*, IMF World Economic and Financial Surveys, October 2010.

Indira Gandhi Institute of Development Research, *Data and Definitions: Underestimating Savings and Investment in an Open Economy*, 2007.

Intergovernmental Panel on Climate Change, *Fourth Assessment Report: Climate Change 2007.*

Jackson, Richard, Neil Howe, with Rebecca Strauss and Keisuke Nakashima, *The Graying of the Great Powers: Demography and Geopolitics in the 21st Century*, Washington, DC: CSIS Press, 2008.

Jackson, Richard, Neil Howe, with Rebecca Strauss and Keisuke Nakashima, *China's Long March to Retirement Reform: The Graying of the Middle Kingdom Revisited*, Washington, DC: CSIS Press, 2009.

Jackson, Richard, Neil Howe, and Keisuke Nakashima, *The global aging preparedness index*, Center for Strategic & International Studies (CSIS), October 2010.

Jain-Chandra, Sonali, and Marcos Chamon, *Access to finance and household consumption*, presentation, IMF, Beijing, January 21, 2010.

Jenkinson, Tim, "Regulation and the cost of capital," in Michael Crew and David Parker, eds., *International Handbook on Economic Regulation*, Northampton, MA: Edward Elgar Publishing, 2006.

Jha, Shikha, Eswar Prasad, and Akiko Terada-Hagiwara, "Saving in Asia and issues for rebalancing growth," ADB economics working paper 162, Asian Development Bank, May 2009.

Kamin, Steven B., "Financial globalization and monetary policy," Board of Governors of the Federal Reserve System International Finance discussion paper 1002, June 2010.

Khoman, Ehsan, and Martin Weale, *Are we living beyond our means? A comparison of France, Italy, Spain, and the United Kingdom*, National Institute of Economic and Social Research, April 2008.

Koller, Tim, Richard Dobbs, and Bill Huyett, *Value: The Four Cornerstones of Corporate Finance*, Hoboken, NJ: Wiley, 2010.

Lequiller, François, and Derek Blades, *Understanding National Accounts*, OECD, 2006.

Lusardi, Annamaria, Jonathan Skinner, and Steven Venti, "Saving puzzles and saving policies in the United States," *Oxford Review of Economic Policy*, Volume 17, Number 1, October 2003.

Ma, Guonan, and Wang Yi, "China's high saving rate: Myth and reality," BIS working paper 312, June 2010.

Madisson, Angus, "A long-run perspective on saving," *Scandinavian Journal of Economics*, June 1992.

Mankiw, N. Gregory, David Romer, and David N. Weil, "A contribution to the empirics of economic growth," *The Quarterly Journal of Economics*, Volume 107, Number 2, May 1992.

McKinsey & Company, *Pathways to a low-carbon economy; Version 2 of the global greenhouse gas abatement cost curve*, 2009.

McKinsey & Company, *Two trillion and counting: Assessing the credit gap for small- and medium-sized enterprises in the developing world*, October 2010.

McKinsey Global Institute, *The coming demographic deficit: How aging populations will reduce global savings*, January 2005.

McKinsey Global Institute, *Accelerating India's growth through financial system reform*, June 2006.

McKinsey Global Institute, *Preparing for China's urban billion*, March 2008.

McKinsey Global Institute, *Talkin' 'bout my generation: The economic impact of aging US baby boomers*, June 2008.

McKinsey Global Institute, *Will US consumer debt reduction cripple the recovery?*, March 2009.

McKinsey Global Institute, *The new power brokers: How oil, Asia, hedge funds, and private equity are faring in the financial crisis*, July 2009.

McKinsey Global Institute, *If you've got it, spend it: Unleashing the Chinese consumer*, August 2009.

McKinsey Global Institute, *Global capital markets: Entering a new era*, September 2009.

McKinsey Global Institute, *Debt and deleveraging: The global credit bubble and its economic consequences*, January 2010.

McKinsey Global Institute, *India's urban awakening: Building inclusive cities, sustaining economic growth*, April 2010.

McKinsey Global Institute, *Growth and competitiveness in the United States: The role of its multinational companies*, June 2010.

McKinsey Global Institute, *Beyond austerity: A path to economic growth and renewal in Europe*, October 2010.

McKinsey Global Institute, *Beyond the downturn: Securing long-term UK growth*, November 2010.

McQuinn, Kieran, and Karl Whelan, "Conditional convergence and the dynamics of the capital-output ratio," *Journal of Economic Growth*, Volume 12, Number 2, 2007.

"Measuring the Balassa-Samuelson effect for the countries of Central and Eastern Europe?," *Banque de France Bulletin Digest*, Number 122, February 2004.

Ministry of Statistics and Programme Implementation, Government of India, *Report of the High Level Committee on Estimation of Saving and Investment*, 2009.

Modigliani, Franco, and Shi Larry Cao, "The Chinese saving puzzle and the life-cycle hypothesis," *Journal of Economic Literature*, Volume 42, March 2004.

Mohan, Rakesh, "Economic reforms and corporate performance in India," special talk at Federation of Indian Chambers of Commerce & Industry (FICCI-IBA) Conference, Global Banking: Paradigm Shift, September 14, 2007.

Mohan, Rakesh, "The future of financial regulation: Some reflections," R. K. Talwar Memorial discussion paper, July 28, 2010.

Muellbauer, John, *Housing, credit and consumer expenditure*, Center for Economic Policy Research (CEPR), April 2008.

Nair, Lekshmi R., "Financial sector liberalization and household savings in India," Indian Institute of Capital Markets 9th Capital Markets Conference Paper, January 2006.

Nishikawa, Yukio, *India: Higher saving rate holds the key to a sustained growth*, Japan Center for Economic Research staff report, January 25, 2007.

Obstfeld, Maurice, and Kenneth Rogoff, *Global imbalances and the financial crisis: Products of common causes*, prepared for the Federal Reserve Bank of San Francisco's Asia Economic Policy Conference, October 2009.

OECD, "Fiscal implications of ageing: Projections of age-related spending," *OECD Economic Outlook*, chapter IV, Number 69, 2001.

OECD, "Projecting OECD health and long-term care expenditures: What are the main drivers?" working paper 477, 2006.

OECD, "Corporate saving and investment: Recent trends and prospects," *OECD Economic Outlook*, chapter III, Number 82, 2008.

OECD, *Economic Outlook*, Number 87, 2010.

Officer, Lawrence, and Samuel Williamson, "Annual Inflation Rates in the United States, 1775-2009, and United Kingdom, 1265-2009," *MeasuringWorth*, 2009.

Ogawa, Kazuo, "Why did Japan's household savings rate fall in the 1990s?," Institute of Social and Economic Research discussion paper 632, March 2005.

Ostry, Jonathan D., Atish R. Ghosh, Jun I. Kim, and Mahvash S. Qureshi, "Fiscal Space," IMF Research Department staff position note, September 2010.

Parry, Martin, Nigel Arnell, Pam Berry, David Dodman, Samuel Fankhauser, Chris Hope, Sari Kovats, Robert Nicolls, David Satterwaite, Richard Tiffin, and Tim Wheeler, *Assessing the Costs of Adaptation to Climate Change: A Review of the UNFCCC and Other Recent Estimates*, International Institute for Environment and Development (UK) and the Grantham Institute for Climate Change, Imperial College, London, UK, August 2009.

Pensions Commission, *Implementing an integrated package of pension reforms: The final report of the Pensions Commission*, 2006.

Poterba, James, *International Comparisons of Household Saving*, Chicago: University of Chicago Press, 1994.

Poterba, James, "The impact of population aging on financial markets," NBER working paper 10851, October 2004.

Poterba, James, Steven Venti, and David A. Wise, "New estimates of the future path of 401(k) assets," NBER working paper 13083, May 2007.

Qiao, Helen, and Yu Song, "China's savings rate and its long-term outlook," Goldman Sachs Global Economics working paper 191, 2009.

Rajan, Raghuram G., *Fault Lines: How Hidden Fractures Still Threaten the World Economy*, Princeton, New Jersey: Princeton University Press, 2010.

Reinhardt, Nola, "The conundrum of low saving rates in Latin America," *Development Policy Review*, Volume 26, Number 6, November 2008.

Reinsdorf, Marshall B., "Alternative measures of personal saving," *Survey of Current Business*, February 2007.

Riddick, Leigh A., and Toni M. Whited, "The corporate propensity to save," *The Journal of Finance*, Volume 64, Number 4, August 2009.

Samuelson, Paul A., "Theoretical notes on trade problems," *Review of Economics and Statistics*, Volume 46, Number 2, May 1964.

Shin, Hyun Song, "Risk and Liquidity: Clarendon Lectures in Finance," June 2010

Standard & Poor's, *Global Aging 2010: An Irreversible Truth*, October 7, 2010.

Stein, Peer, Tony Goland, and Robert Schiff, *Two trillion and counting: Assessing the gap for micro, small, and medium-sized enterprises in the developing world*, McKinsey & Company and the World Bank Group International Finance Corporation, October 2010.

Steindel, Charles, "How worrisome is a negative saving rate?," Federal Reserve Bank of New York, *Current Issues in Economics and Finance*, Volume 13, Number 4, May 2007.

Taki, Toshio, "Household financial assets in Japan: 2007 in retrospect," *Nomura Capital Market Review*, Volume 11, Number 2, April 2008.

Taylor, John B., *Getting Off Track: How Government Actions and Interventions Caused, Prolonged, and Worsened the Financial Crisis*, Palo Alto, California: Hoover Institution Press, 2009.

Terrones, Marco, and Roberto Cardarelli, "Global imbalances: A saving and investment perspective," *World Economic Outlook 2005 of the International Monetary Fund*.

Tett, Gillian, *Fool's Gold: How Unrestrained Greed Corrupted a Dream, Shattered Global Markets and Unleashed a Catastrophe*, New York: Free Press, 2010.

Thorne, Susie, and Jill Cropp, "Household saving in Australia," The Treasury of the Australian Government, *Economic Roundup*, Issue 4, 2008.

Turner, Adair, "What do banks do, what should they do and what public policies are needed to ensure best results for the real economy?", speech delivered at CASS Business School, March 17, 2010.

US Department of Transportation of the United States, *2006 Status of the Nation's Highways, Bridges, and Transit: Conditions and Performance*, 2006.

Warnock, Francis E. "How dangerous is US government debt? The risks of a sudden spike in US interest rates," *Capital Flows Quarterly*, Council on Foreign Relations (CFR), June 2010.

Wilson, Dominic, and Swarnali Ahmed, "Current accounts and demographics: The road ahead," Goldman Sachs Global Economics, Commodities and Strategy Research working paper 202, August 2010.

Wolf, Martin, *Fixing Global Finance*, Baltimore: Johns Hopkins University Press, September 2008.

World Bank Group, *The Economics of Adaptation to Climate Change*, August 2010.

World Bank Group International Finance Corporation, *Scaling-up SME Access to Financial Services in the Developing World*, released at the G-20 Seoul Summit, November 2010.

Recent McKinsey Global Institute publications

October 2010
Beyond austerity: A path to economic growth and renewal in Europe

With multiple pressures on growth and constrained public finances, Europe needs structural reform even to match past GDP growth rates. Parts of Europe have begun to reform with demonstrable success. If the rest of Europe emulated their best practice, the region could add 4 to 11 percent to per capita GDP, without cutting holidays and leave.

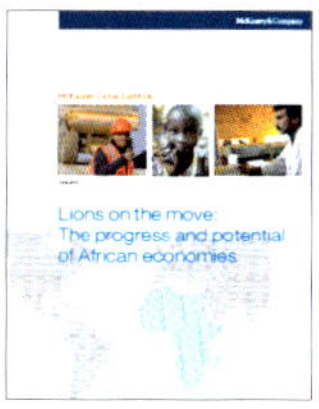

June 2010
Lions on the move: The progress and potential of African economies

Africa's economic growth is creating substantial new business opportunities that are often overlooked by global companies. Consumer-facing industries, resources, agriculture, and infrastructure together could generate as much as $2.6 trillion in revenue annually by 2020, or $1 trillion more than today.

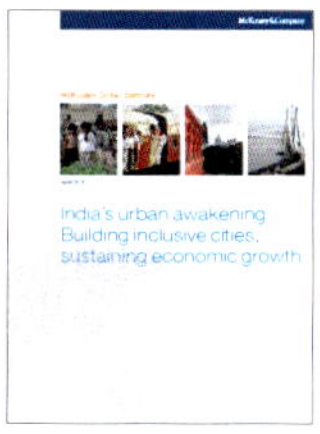

April 2010
India's urban awakening: Building inclusive cities, sustaining economic growth

India's lack of effective policies to manage its rapid and large-scale urbanization could jeopardize the nation's growth trajectory. But if India pursues a new operating model for its cities, it could add as much as 1 to 1.5 percent to annual GDP growth.

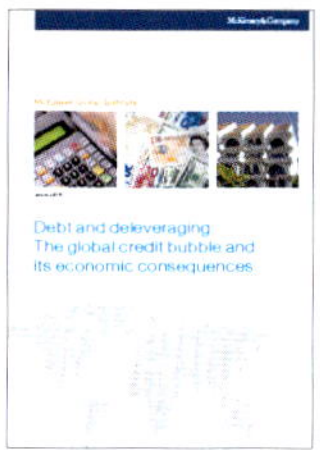

January 2010
Debt and deleveraging: The global credit bubble and its economic consequences

The recent bursting of the great global credit bubble left a large burden of debt weighing on many households, businesses, and governments around the world. Leverage levels are still high in ten sectors of five major economies. If history is a guide, one would expect many years of debt reduction in these sectors, which would exert a significant drag on GDP growth.

August 2009
If you've got it, spend it: Unleashing the Chinese consumer

By pursuing a more aggressive reform program, China's leaders could raise private consumption above 50 percent of GDP by 2025, vaulting China's economy into a new phase.

September 2009
Global capital markets: Entering a new era

World financial assets fell by $16 trillion to $178 trillion in 2008, marking the largest setback on record. Looking ahead, mature financial markets may be headed for slower growth, while emerging markets will likely account for an increasing share of global asset growth.

www.mckinsey.com/mgi

eBook versions of selected MGI reports are available on MGI's website, on Amazon's Kindle bookstore, and on Apple's iBookstore.

Download and listen to MGI podcasts on iTunes or at
http://www.mckinsey.com/mgi/publications/multimedia/

Made in United States
North Haven, CT
04 November 2026

21725773R00060